how to develop a winning personality

Martin Panzer

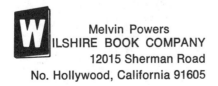

Melvin Powers
WILSHIRE BOOK COMPANY
12015 Sherman Road
No. Hollywood, California 91605

MANUFACTURED IN THE UNITED STATES OF AMERICA

ISBN 0-87980-057-7

Contents

INTRODUCTION   9

I. YOU'RE NOT THE ONLY ONE   13

The personality deficiencies that cause loneliness . . . How much loneliness is too much? . . . Fundamental approach to conquest of loneliness.

II. GETTING TO KNOW YOURSELF   22

Analyzing your own personality . . . Measuring your estimate of your own worth . . . How to tell whether you are too modest or too conceited . . . How to find factors in your personality that repel or attract . . . How others see you.

III. REJECTED? BLAME YOURSELF   40

You are valued by others according to the value you set on yourself . . . The need to be brutally frank with yourself . . . How to react to attributes or events that cannot be changed or undone . . . The indispensability of sharing . . . The crime of selling yourself short.

IV. A MILLION WAYS TO MEET NEW PEOPLE   62

Eliminating your personal iron curtain . . . Formula for getting people to pay special attention to you . . . New methods for meeting people and drawing them into your life . . . Evolving other methods of your own.

V. MAKE YOURSELF COLORFUL   89

The most important ingredient of the colorful personality . . . The use of "gimmicks" in creating personality magnetism . . .

The gimmicks of famous people . . . The importance of curiosity and the sin of nosiness . . . How to be direct without being obnoxious . . . The value of knowing what you want.

VI. SKELETONS IN YOUR CLOSET 110

The tragic consequences of trying to hide shortcomings or the less happy facts about yourself and your life . . . The inhibiting influence on your personality of "keeping people out" . . . How to free your personality of inhibiting elements.

VII. DON'T LIVE ALONE IF YOU DON'T LIKE IT 122

The problems of living alone . . . Various ways of sharing your home life.

VIII. BOY MEETS GIRL 140

How to make a date . . . The two major elements of dating . . . How to make sure of repeat dates: four basic personality attributes that assure the success of the first date.

IX. WHAT TO DO WHEN CUPID GOES 155

How to alleviate the effects of a broken heart or a divorce on your personality . . . Guarding against new hurts . . . Minimizing the damage and capitalizing on experience.

X. GIVE YOURSELF AWAY 170

The personality magnetism that results from dedication to a cause . . . How to get involved in a cause . . . Raising your standard in the community . . . Career advancement as a by-product of doing good.

XI. YOUR NEIGHBORS ARE NICE PEOPLE 187

Your neighbors are a reflection of yourself . . . Personality requirements for being a good neighbor . . . Advantages of neighborhood life . . . What neighbors ask of you and what they give in return.

XII. Must You Leave? Here's Your Hat   202

How to be a good host and how to be a good guest . . . The basic elements of entertaining in your home . . . The rewards of a reputation as a good host . . . How to decide the best way for you to entertain . . . How to be a much-desired guest . . . What gifts to bring, what to talk about, what to ask for, how to behave, when to go.

XIII. Eight Hours a Day   227

The personality requirements of the good colleague at office or shop . . . How to get to like "going to work" even though you may not like the work itself . . . Analyzing yourself as a colleague . . . What to do to make your colleagues like you.

XIV. I'd Climb the Highest Mountain   236

Measuring your capacity for friendship . . . How many friends an individual can have . . . The burdens and the joys of friendship . . . Why you need at least one friend to have a rounded personality . . . How to hold a friend . . . How to make a new friend.

XV. Your Best Friend Is You   244

How to be self-sufficient . . . How to organize your time so you can enjoy and learn from the myriad interests available in the twentieth century . . . Developing the art of conversation . . . How to read . . . The development of taste in the arts . . . Taking advantage of the world's treasures to make yourself a fully rounded personality.

Introduction

❧ Are you a saint or a genius? If you are one or the other I would suggest that you return this book to the shop and get your money back. You'll get by if you are completely minus personality in the sense that the word is commonly used: the image you project as a social being. A saint will be loved for his goodness even if he is a hermit and a genius will be sought after and admired for his accomplishments even if he is an ill-mannered grouch.

I suspect, however, that you are neither a saint nor a genius and that your personality is a matter of great concern to you as it is to the rest of us ordinary folk. This is rather a sad state of affairs. It would be a much better world if we were judged and sought after for whatever little goodness we manifested and for whatever small talents we possessed.

Things were different in days gone by. You didn't have to ooze charm, for instance, to be elected President of the United States or to be promoted from the stock room to the executive office. It wasn't necessary to be an enthralling conversationalist to win friends or to be a glamor girl to get a boy friend. Intrinsic merit was the yardstick by which others judged you.

This is not to say that personality was not a useful characteristic even then. As far back as 1871 Walt Whitman wrote that "it is native personality that endows a man to stand before presidents or generals, or in any distinguished collection, with *aplomb*—and *not* culture, or any knowledge or intellect whatever." Nevertheless, you will note that Whitman made it clear that the personality kid was not a general or a president or anyone important but only one who could stand among important people with aplomb.

Those days are over. Not only could Abraham Lincoln, one of the greatest men of all time, not have been elected President in the space and television age—he could not even have been nominated. The image makers and measurers would have ruled him out before he got started. We live in the age of personality and, as practical people, we must adjust to it. If it's personality they want, let's give it to them.

Actually, if you don't let it get in the way of your decency and ability, personality is a pleasant thing to have.

It is personality for its own sake, personality as an exclusive goal, personality as an obsession that is a minus quantity —the personality (in Whitman's words) without culture, without knowledge and without intellect.

With these reservations in mind, it is entirely commendable to devote some thought and effort to the improvement of your personality. You do not have to make it the be all and end all of your existence but you can and should, as a normal human being, make enough concession to space-age attitudes to be able to live comfortably and happily in the space age. If you don't, and if you are not a saint or a genius, you are going to be a mighty lonely soul, and that brings us to one of the major—if not *the* major—reasons for devoting yourself in at least a limited way to the improvement and development of your personality.

Our approach will be sensible rather than inspiring. Our aim will be practical rather than ambitious. In these pages you will not find the road to success through personality. What you *may* find, if you do most of the work yourself, is the way to make the most of your natural gifts —the way to go from loneliness to companionship and contentment—the way to become a part of the seething life about you and to be no longer apart from it. The way, in short, to become a personable human being to whom others turn for friendship as they offer friendship in return.

And if, as you progress along this way, it should lead you to some material profit and advancement, just consider it an unintended bonus. After all, this is also the age of the chain reaction.

Chapter One

YOU'RE NOT THE ONLY ONE

Are you looking forward with dread to the moment when you must go to bed tonight? That's the moment when lonely people are at their loneliest—when the emptiness of living seems to bear down on body and soul with oppressive vividness, like a living, breathing monster whose one aim is to shut you off from the warmth and the softness and the love and the understanding of all of the other people in the world. That's the moment you feel most sorry for yourself; nor can anyone blame you for your self-pity.

Well, here's a comforting thought to take to bed with you: You've got plenty of company in your loneliness; the world is teeming with lonely people. And here's a thought that's even more comforting: Loneliness is not necessarily chronic or incurable.

The fact is, everybody is alone in this world to a greater or lesser degree. Have you, for example, ever been able to be so *together* with another human being, however dear to you, however intimate with you, that you really knew him: his thoughts, his doubts, his dreams, his reactions, his fears? If you are naïve enough to believe that you have, suppose we put it another way: have you ever permitted anyone in the world really and truly to know you —the you that you are in the deep recesses of your heart?

There is in you an area of reserve that belongs to you and God alone; it is when that area of reserve grows greater than you can bear without aching that your loneliness becomes tragic. Before that, loneliness is an opportunity for communion . . . with yourself . . . with God.

Unfortunately, loneliness too often reaches out beyond the normal, healthful area of reserve into the area of aching emptiness. The fundamental secret of the cure for loneliness is the ability to regulate adequately the size of the area of reserve so that it is just exactly right for the individual concerned; and that is what we shall attempt to help you do in the pages that follow.

So many of us are so lonely so much of the time! Whole industries have sprung up whose mission, in whole or in part, is to soothe the ache and fill the emptiness when the understanding heart we seek has not been found. Lonely hearts clubs and pen pal clubs cover the land. Music schools and dance studios assure us we'll never be lonely again if we but learn to play an instrument and to dance.

Beauty and charm experts and cosmetic manufacturers and deodorant makers and toothpaste blenders and soap mixers and public-speaking coaches and evening schools and seashore hotels all hold out to us that great and precious boon: release from loneliness.

The trouble is that they all make the same mistake: they sell us a cure from without but fail first to prepare us from within. The best anti-loneliness remedy—and many of the remedies offered are valuable—is useless, or worse than useless, if we are not ready for it. For instance: what will it profit you to learn to dance if as you dance the ache of loneliness still fills you through and through? And what good is it to look lovely and to smell clean if your heart is empty? If there is one thing the lonely ones know it is that you can't measure another man's loneliness by the number of people who may be sharing a city, a street, a house or even a room with him.

But if you have just one other human being who provides for you the togetherness you need, then the dancing and the playing and the learning and the beautifying all take on new and delicious meaning. And to have even one person in the world like that, you have to be able to be a person like that for him. In other words, you can't cure your own loneliness until you are able to take some loneliness out of someone else's life.

Isn't it an odd thing—a sensationally odd thing—that the only emotion in your whole range of emotions that you cannot share is your loneliness? The very act of sharing, sharing anything at all, even unbeknownst to the person with whom you share—even a thought in the back reaches of your mind—is a negation of loneliness, for loneliness and sharing simply do not mix. Even if you made a conscious effort to share your loneliness you would, in the process, kill it at least a little bit.

That is why it is so important for you to be aware that so many other people are lonely. Just sharing the knowledge of the loneliness of others is comforting because you do not feel so alone when you know that so many other men and women are lonely. If misery loves company, many of us have a lot of company to love, for the incidence of loneliness in our population is greater than the incidence of all other illnesses of the spirit combined. The billions of dollars spent each year on the anti-loneliness miracle drugs mentioned above are proof enough that this is so.

Down through the ages the virtues and the vices of solitude have engaged the thoughts of the poets and the sages. If Milton cried out that "loneliness is the first thing which God's eye named not good," there was Balzac to protest: "We must certainly acknowledge that solitude is a fine thing." And when Thoreau wrote: "I love to be alone. I never found the companion that was so companionable as solitude," he was contradicted by the French poet Méry, who felt that "solitude is the worst of all companions."

Let the poets and sages battle it out. Perhaps all of them are right for the moment in which they write. When loneliness crowds in on us with all its aching emptiness we are altogether in the camp of Milton and Méry. And yet, there must be moments of loneliness in the life of every man to make him rise to his own inimitable, incomparable, unique status in the universe.

In that fountain of Hebrew wisdom, the Talmud, it is written that man was not intended to live alone but as a member of society . . . that an isolated life would not be worth living . . . that the desirability of comradeship is deduced from Ecclesiastes: "Two are better than one, because they have a good reward for their labor. For if they fall, the one will lift up his fellow: but woe to him that is alone when he falleth: for he hath not another to help him up."

If this preoccupation carries back beyond the poets to the days of the Bible itself, one must assume that it is more or less an integral part of life as we know it. This may be due in part to man's natural fear of the dangers that beset him from the moment he is born. The one-day-old infant, weeping pitifully, will suddenly cease from weeping when his mother holds him to her. Who can tell what the little mind fears: a fall—hunger—thirst—or even aloneness itself? "But woe to him that is alone when he falleth; for he hath not another to pick him up."

Later there are the thunder and the lightning; the wind and the hail; the beasts of the forest; the enemy tribe . . . and through the long vistas of history all of the known and unknown dangers down to the H-bomb of our own enlightened day. And every time, before he was able to conquer the dangers that arose, man maintained his composure, his very sanity, by huddling together with his fellow men.

As he progressed, he found more in comradeship than mere comfort and safety. He learned to like and then to love the presence and the understanding of others. He felt, when he was alone, not the fear that he would not have "another to help him up," but rather an aching emptiness because he did not have another to love and understand him—that ill we know as loneliness.

It is clear, therefore, that the capacity for loneliness in the sense in which we speak of it is a measure of the degree to which the human animal has risen above the beasts of the forest, the farm and the hearth. The animals that huddle together do so for good and sufficient reasons: the herds and the coveys and the schools and the flocks are nature's design for animal living, survival and propagation. The bear cub misses the mother bear because it craves the food and the warmth and the security she can provide. Only for you and your fellow human beings, however, does loneliness have a profoundly unselfish and unmaterialistic basis.

Indeed, association with man may sometimes make even a beast rise to that higher form of loneliness. The dog that pines and starves for days at the foot of his dead master's grave is an animal that has been touched by a human soul and has learned from the touch what it means to be truly lonely.

This is not to sing in praise of loneliness but rather to point out that your loneliness is not to be considered a source of shame or a reason for self-reproach. Your capacity for loneliness is something in which you should feel pride even at the moment when you strive, rightly, to vanquish it.

There may be some who will dispute the claim that all men are to some degree lonely and that this should attach no blame to them. They will say that if a man believes in God he can never feel alone. This is an argument for which there can be no refutation if one accepts the premise that togetherness with other human beings can be equated with togetherness with God. But if one accepts the premise that togetherness with God does not preclude a very deep need for togetherness with others of God's children, one can go forward to the cure of loneliness as the cure of something which exists and whose existence casts no blame or shame on its victims.

There may be others who will say that if a man has within himself the resources that make him a whole man, he can never be lonely, for among those resources are sufficient outlets for his interest, his occupation and his emotional involvement to keep him from missing the companionship of other men. It was Montaigne who said, indeed, that "Nature has presented us with a large faculty of entertaining ourselves alone, and often calls us to it, to teach us that we owe ourselves in part to society, but chiefly and mostly to ourselves."

There is much to be said for this philosophy, selfish as it may sound; one of the aims of this book will be to help you develop the faculty of entertaining yourself alone.

We have already indicated that loneliness is not a matter of mere physical togetherness or the lack of it; that a man can be more lonely in a room full of people than in an empty room. Togetherness does not require physical presence, but the lack of physical presence can lead to loneliness for those who lack the faculty of "entertaining themselves alone" and thereby enjoying, with complete lack of loneliness, their togetherness with absent ones.

But here is the paradox of the philosophy of Montaigne and his disciples: the men who are whole, who have a large faculty of entertaining themselves, usually have to struggle to find opportunities for being alone, because their company is so attractive to other people! And by the same token, those who do not have the faculty of entertaining themselves seem always to lack the faculty of entertaining others, so that their loneliness is compounded. In brief, the advice of Montaigne is wasted because those who are able to take it do not need it.

We come now to the vital question: Why are so many people so lonely so much of the time?

There is no single reason; as a matter of fact there are countless reasons, of which perhaps the most common are the following: the feeling of being misunderstood; the necessity for taking responsibility for great decisions; the problems and mysteries of adolescence; the fears and adjustments of aging; the loss of loved ones; the lack of brothers and sisters; shyness and self-consciousness; change in matrimonial status; spinsterhood and bachelorhood; social and intellectual inadequacy; lack of fixed goal or purpose; physical handicaps; separation from home and family; removal to a new neighborhood or country; economic unsuccessfulness; minority status; lack of demonstrativeness; being without fixed goal or purpose; chronic self-pity—to record only a few.

You can boil down all of these reasons and most of those omitted to one cover-all: personality deficiencies. It goes back to our comments about space-age attitudes in the Introduction to this volume. People look for personality rather than intrinsic merit. They no longer have the time or patience or desire to worry about your troubles. Unless you have a bit of magnetism they won't even bother to visit you when you are sick in a hospital. It is not that they are bad or selfish; they are merely caught up in the swirl of our hectic age and have become thoughtless. As a rule they do what they like to do. And if they like to be with you, you won't be lonely whatever your problems may be.

Chapter Two

GETTING TO KNOW YOURSELF

❦ In this chapter we are going to analyze your personality and see whether or not you may be suffering from some weaknesses that may be serving to repel rather than to attract the people about you. Before we get to that, however, let us examine one facet of your total mental attitude on which your major social strength must rest —that is, your opinion of yourself.

You should be able honestly to think of yourself as someone pretty special. You may have this feeling of self-esteem even if, as you may find on ensuing pages, there are certain negative features in your personality. The correction of the negative features will then serve to add legitimacy and force to your respect for yourself.

You know, to yourself you are probably the ideal companion, for in your own company there is no conflict of tastes, dreams, ambitions, dislikes, loves or fears. Shakespeare said: "I to myself am dearer than a friend." Confucius said it even more emphatically: "What the superior man seeks is in himself; what the small man seeks is in others."

Look at the world about you; see the men who lead us, who lead the peoples of the world—the men who accomplish—the men who influence. They make mistakes. They sometimes make enemies. Often they are foolish. But always they hold themselves high in esteem—high enough to believe that what they do, what they think, what they advocate, is right.

More important to your present need than this knowledge itself is the fact that when you begin to appreciate yourself, something rather wonderful happens to your personality. If your self-esteem is not a fraud—if it is based on genuine worth—it sends out waves of attraction that draw the esteem and the interest of others to you. The great trick is to keep from going beyond self-esteem to conceit, which is more damaging than excess modesty.

As Hazlitt pointed out: "Let a man's talents and virtues be what they may, we only feel satisfaction in his society as he is satisfied in himself"; and as he warned on another occasion: "Conceit is the most contemptible and one of the most odious qualities in the world." There is a line between self-appreciation and conceit, and it is the height of self-discipline to stop as close to that line as possible.

There can, of course, be no scientific measurement of

your self-esteem, any more than there can be such measurement of any of your personality traits. And yet we can establish a rule of thumb by which to measure these intangibles with sufficient approximate accuracy to render them valid. The best such rule of thumb is the questionnaire which gives you an opportunity to estimate the degree of your inclination toward a given weakness or a given strength.

The following questionnaire may, in some sections, appear to you to be irrelevant to the subject of self-esteem, but our personality weak points and strong points need not always be measured by reference to a particular trait which may be under discussion. For instance, it took years of experience in the development of the study of psychology to bring psychologists to the point of declaring that when a baby brushes his lips with a blanket he is seeking and finding a form of security. If you didn't first give the matter much thought there would seem to be very little relationship to fear in the feel of a blanket.

As we grow older and begin to understand the direct relationship between our actions and our personality weaknesses, we begin to hide these weaknesses when they are sufficiently obvious for us to recognize them. Thus, a man who fears heights may train himself to avoid reference to his fear. To make this easier, he may even manage to avoid heights. If that is not possible, he may force himself not to look from high windows or out of planes. He may come to disguise his fear so well that his friends may never become aware of it. He may come in time to set up a block against his own recognition (conscious) of his fear. If you were to ask him directly if he were afraid of heights he might truthfully say no.

Nevertheless, a psychologist might, through a series of questions, discover his fear without ever mentioning it directly, because incident to the fear itself there would be revealing factors. There might be recurrent dreams of falling. There might be a revulsion to tall women. There might be a distrust of the brakes of automobiles. There might be an exaggerated love for the seashore as a vacation place. There might be an antipathy to birds. There might be a hundred and one other things, no one or two or three of them overly significant, none of them related directly to fear of heights, but in the aggregate more or less conclusive proof of such fear.

We are ready, then, for our first self-examination.

ARE YOU CONVINCED OF YOUR OWN WORTH?

Credit yourself with five points for each answer which can honestly be "No." If you run up a score of seventy or more, you have sufficient self-esteem to disregard this subject as a contributing factor in your loneliness. If your score is very low, say forty or less, you may reasonably conclude that the task of bringing it higher is more important than anything else in your effort to defeat loneliness. If you are not a friend even to yourself in this sense, you are twice lonely. You will probably find that the very discovery of the problem you face is a vital first step toward overcoming it.

1. Do you ever have the feeling that no one really worth while could fall in love with you?
2. Do you always take someone with you when you buy wearing apparel?
3. Is it impossible or extremely difficult for you to ask for a raise?
4. When another driver sounds his horn in criticism of your driving, do you slow down to let him pass you?
5. Do you permit people who enter a store after your own entrance to push ahead of you for service?
6. Do you yield when others express forceful opinions, though you may continue to disagree mentally?
7. Do you belong to fan clubs; do you collect autographs of current celebrities?
8. Are you unceasingly concerned about your complexion, or body odor, or the color of your teeth, etc.?
9. Are you overly modest about your own efforts or accomplishments?
10. When you receive change, do you pocket it without counting it?
11. Do you always apologize for your dancing?
12. Do you allow others at the office or shop to pass the buck to you?

13. Are you an easy mark for a salesman?

14. Are you excessively punctual?

15. Do you tip too generously?

16. Are you jealous?

17. Do you need a drink or two before you can "open up" in company?

18. Do you cater or kowtow to others?

19. Are you always the last of your party to enter a taxi?

20. Are you unduly hesitant about inconveniencing others—for instance, are you afraid to make rustling sounds or move about in your seat at the theatre; do you eat foods you don't like or can't stomach just to be agreeable, etc.?

We shall cross the line from self-esteem to conceit only as an intellectual exercise because, though self-esteem and conceit are always in danger of merging at one point or another, conceit is hardly a weakness that will result in loneliness. Those who are conceited are too enamored of themselves to miss togetherness with others, though in rare moments of self-revelation they may have sudden loneliness pangs; nothing repels more effectively than conceit.

It is hardly likely that you would be reading a book like this if you were genuinely conceited, but accidents will happen and if the next questionnaire should by some strange chance point the finger at you, you would be well-advised to draw back more closely to the fine dividing line between honorable self-esteem and obnoxious conceit.

Are You Conceited?

If you score over sixty-five points, counting five for each "Yes" answer, you are too madly in love with yourself. If you gather between forty-five and sixty points, you are still your own sweetheart. If your score is under forty-five, you could become likable with very little extra effort.

1. Are you habitually critical and fault-finding?
2. Do you refuse to take anybody's advice?
3. Do you stick dogmatically to your arguments in the face of all disproof?
4. When you travel about with others do you always expect the entire group to do what you want to do?
5. Does it upset you when someone forgets your name?
6. Do you spend more than the average amount of time on your personal appearance; do you look into the mirror frequently?
7. Do you often interrupt others when they speak?
8. When someone tells a joke do you only half listen while preparing to tell another story as soon as he has finished?
9. Do many people bore you?
10. Do you sign your name with numerous flourishes?
11. Do you refuse to ask for directions when you are uncertain of your route?

12. Is your manner toward waiters and others overbearing?
13. Are you often sarcastic?
14. Are you what is known as a sore loser?
15. Do you sulk if you are not the center of attention?
16. When you make a wager, do you usually offer very high odds?
17. Do you habitually carry large sums of cash on your person?
18. Do you hog the road or the conversation?
19. Do you like to sit in box seats?
20. Are you ever ashamed of your parents or other relatives?

Beyond the basic weakness of lack of self-esteem (or, of course, too much self-esteem), there are secondary habits and attitudes which can stand in the way of establishing friendship or even acquaintanceship with others and thus contribute to loneliness. I do not speak of trite and oftmentioned deficiencies such as rudeness, ignorance, sloppiness, bigotry, crudity, dishonesty, etc., which repel rather than attract. We can hardly be expected to sympathize with those who are lonely because of such unworthy traits, for such traits are usually within the realm of the conscious, and therefore usually inexcusable.

I refer, rather, to what I consider to be innocent, unconscious shortcomings which lead to the same punishing loneliness. These are rarely discussed and even more rarely known or understood by those affected by them. If any of them apply to you, the fact may easily be brought out through the questionnaires that follow. As we have indicated, there can be nothing strictly scientific about such questionnaires and so we shall eliminate the scoring systems. You will be able to get an adequate picture of your own personality as related to the specific problems discussed merely by applying the measurement of common sense to your answers.

Do You Put People on the Spot?

Quite innocently you may be guilty of consistently embarrassing people by putting them, so to speak, on the spot. You may do this in ways that may seem perfectly harmless to you and, indeed, if you don't do it often, they are fairly harmless. It is the habit of making people *repeatedly* uncomfortable that eventually leads them to try to avoid your company.

I know one girl, for instance, who wouldn't for the world intentionally embarrass anyone. However, she thinks nothing at all of saying, "May I borrow your comb? I've forgotten my own." Many people don't like the idea of having others use their combs. They may hand their combs over without saying anything, even if they are impelled to throw them away later, but you may be certain the experience will not induce them to seek out the company of the borrowers in the future.

The point is that you've got to be sure of your ground before you can permit yourself to be utterly spontaneous.

If you have a modicum of horse sense you know very well where and in what company you can be your own full, free self and where you cannot. It might be perfectly permissible for you to ask an intimate friend to lend you a comb and it might be completely out of order to make the same request of a mere acquaintance.

With this understanding, we may proceed to the questions:

1. When visiting, do you stay very late?
2. Do you ask casual acquaintances to vouch for your credit or to send letters of reference in your behalf?
3. Do you ask people to recommend doctors to you? (Doctors are sworn to a secret relationship with their patients, but some folks fear that their secrets may inadvertently be released to others.)
4. Do you try to wheedle out secrets?
5. Do you drop in on people without advance notice?
6. When you have a coughing, sneezing cold do you continue to mingle with the people you know?
7. Do you quarrel with husband, wife or sweetheart in the presence of others?
8. Do you ask acquaintances to lend you money?
9. Do you make it a habit to ask people how you look?
10. Do you have to be reminded about money or other things you have borrowed?
11. When you entertain, do you place unusual foods before your guests without ascertaining beforehand whether they like such foods?

12. Do you ask neighbors to mind children or to take care of pets when you go on vacation?

13. Do you show special-occasion gifts to people who have not given you gifts?

14. Do you buy expensive gifts for people who cannot buy such gifts for you?

15. On outings do you suggest entertainment that some members of the party may not be able easily to afford?

16. Do you try to play Cupid to unwilling subjects?

17. Do you ask people to guess how old you are; do you ask people, on the telephone, to guess who you are?

18. Do you ask neighbors to accept department store or other deliveries while you are absent, without regard to their own plans?

19. Do you ever, when you are invited to visit, bring uninvited guests with you?

20. When you plan to ask someone to go out with you, do you start by saying, "What are you doing Saturday night?" (If he says he is free, he may then feel obliged to accept an invitation to do something he would rather not do. The considerate thing to do is to invite the person without that question and permit him to accept or to beg off without feeling put on the spot.)

ARE YOU A BIT OF A STINKER?

This question may shock you but it is nevertheless a fact that you may be one of millions who consider themselves quite nice people but who have certain nasty little habits that make them describable by no other word. More often than not they do the things they do either unconsciously or without realizing that they are earning this unpleasant appellation. It isn't difficult to understand why other people prefer to leave them strictly alone or why loneliness is a part of their lot. If you must answer "Yes" to even a half-dozen of the following questions you would be well-advised to take yourself in hand. Fortunately these habits, which are among the most unpleasant, are among the easiest to eliminate. All that is required is recognition, confession, and the desire for repentance.

1. In crowded shops do you try to get waited on out of turn?
2. Do you start dictating to your secretary at a very late hour in the day?
3. When you have stopped for a light, do you frighten pedestrians by racing your motor when they cross in front of your car?
4. Do you hold long conversations in public telephone booths while others wait impatiently for their turn to use the telephone?
5. Do you park your car so that it "locks in" another car, making it impossible for the owner to extricate it; or do you park so loosely that you use up the space that might enable another driver to park?
6. Do you drop pennies in the basket when charity collections are taken up?

7. Do you mess up the newspaper before the rest of the family gets a chance to read it?

8. Do you tell others the surprise endings of book or movie plots?

9. Do you rest your shod feet on the facing seats in trains?

10. Do you make people ask questions more than once before you deign to answer?

11. Do you tell jokes based on physical or mental handicaps, or racial differences?

12. Do you cough or sneeze in public without using a handkerchief to protect your neighbors?

13. Do you allow your children to go to school when you suspect they are coming down with an illness?

14. Do you keep the overage when a clerk gives you too much change?

15. Do you consider yourself a sharp bargainer?

16. Do you talk in the theatre, at concerts, or at lectures?

17. Do you make sport of drunken men?

18. Do you make busy store clerks show you numerous items when you have no intention of buying anything?

19. In crowded lunchrooms do you remain seated and talking after you have finished your lunch, while others stand by awaiting their turn?

20. Do you play your radio or television loudly in the late hours of the evening?

ARE YOU A WET BLANKET?

Of course you are not! How could you possibly be a wet blanket? A wet blanket is a person whose arrival puts a damper on the party immediately. A wet blanket takes the fun out of everything for everybody. A wet blanket is one of the loneliest people in the world, poor soul, and he never means to be a wet blanket and he never knows he is a wet blanket. Since you couldn't possibly be one of those, don't bother with the following questionnaire. Oh, all right, if you are curious, you may read the questions. But don't blame me for what happens after that. Remember, I said you couldn't possibly be a wet blanket.

1. When you are out for the evening with a group do you complain about the food, the theatre seats, the quality of the show, the cost of the evening, and so on?
2. Does it take a miracle or an earthquake to make you enthusiastic?
3. Do you talk about your operation and your symptoms—are you a hypochondriac?
4. Do you start telling your troubles every time you see an ear?
5. Are you a yes-no-maybe person; is it the hardest thing in the world for you to make up your mind?
6. Are you overly prudish?
7. Is your vocabulary limited to slang or some form of baby talk?

8. Do you brag about your achievements?

9. Are you excessively modest?

10. Do you keep repeating things you have said before?

11. Do you keep referring to the past as the good old days and telling everyone how much better thing were then?

12. Are people afraid to speak freely in your presence because you reveal confidences?

13. Are you a food faddist or a fanatic on any one subject?

14. Do you report to the boss minor infractions by you co-workers?

15. Do you talk shop after business hours?

16. Do you tell people they don't look well, or that they are getting stout, or that they are aging?

17. Are you a go-you-one-better person? That is, i someone catches a big fish do you tell him about bigger one you caught; if he tells you about an an tique he saw do you tell him about an older on you saw; if he tells a joke do you try to top it, etc.

18. Are you a loud talker?

19. Are you a mumbler?

20. Do you always have to get home earlier than th others?

ARE YOU A SPONGER?

Many persons who wouldn't allow anyone to spend dime on them or even to give them a meal might b shocked to learn that they are spongers in less materia but just as unfortunate ways as the money spongers. People like to give, but they don't like to give endlessly and without reciprocation, and when they come across people who sponge on them without letup they find ways and means of making them lonely by avoiding them. How do you shape up in this area of personality deficiency?

1. In conversation, do you leave it to others to do practically all the talking instead of holding up your end of the conversation?
2. Do you always expect people to lunch with you near your office or to visit your home while you turn down similar invitations from them?
3. Do you fail to reply to letters until others have written to you several times?
4. Do you always walk through revolving doors on someone else's push?
5. Do you read newspapers over other people's shoulders?
6. Do you expect your friends to pass on all your clothes before you buy them?
7. Do you prolong telephone conversations that are being paid for by the persons on the other end of the line?
8. Do you make it a practice to ask others to help you with your homework or with your office load?
9. Do you go about without a watch?
10. Do you visit friends at their places of business during business hours?

11. Do you telephone people very late in the evening or very early in the morning?

12. Do you tell very good jokes you have heard to friends of those who told you the jokes, without giving credit?

13. Do you accept compliments without ever returning them?

14. Do you permit husband, wife or sweetheart to make all the amorous advances?

15. Do you offer, as your own, opinions you have heard or read?

16. Are you absent from your job frequently for trivial reasons?

17. Do you use office stationery, stamps, paper clips etc., for your personal needs?

18. Do you permit pets to walk about unleashed on neighbors' property?

19. Do you deduct from your taxes more charitable contributions than you have actually made?

20. Do you permit others to take care of all parent teacher association, civic association and church responsibilities?

Perhaps none, perhaps some, perhaps all of the personality weaknesses highlighted by the above questionnaire may in some measure relate to you. There may very well be others which we have neglected to mention.

It might profit you greatly, now that you have considered the possibility that some of your loneliness may be lue to weaknesses that repel, to set aside two full days on which you will analyze everything you say and everything you do. Consider what your reaction might be if what you were saying and doing were said and done by another.

Chapter Three

REJECTED? BLAME YOURSELF

🌷 From what has already been said here it is clear that your personality, to be whole and magnetic, must project your image in two directions: inward and outward. If you merely make yourself consciously agreeable to others, you will derive little joy, for though it is more blessed to give than to receive, it is not much fun to give without receiving. On the other hand, if you please only yourself, you must inevitably become a narcissist and then you will pine away, like Narcissus, and die of your love for yourself.

In other words, it is necessary for you to direct your personality development toward the conquest of two types of problems: those that trouble you when you are alone and those that trouble you in relationship to others.

For example, the loneliness that is brought on by the

ctual fact of being alone (*viz.*, living alone in an apart-
nent or having no friends in a new place of residence)
alls for remedial action of one sort, while the inability to
raw others to you calls for treatment that is somewhat
ifferent.

Were we to concern ourselves in an exhaustive way
ith all of the personality defects that have loneliness and
ocial inadequacy as by-products, we should have to fill
any volumes. Even if we were prepared to fill the vol-
mes, we would require the assistance of psychologists,
ychiatrists, medical doctors, philosophers, marriage and
ocational counselors and attorneys-at-law, and in addi-
on we should have to arrange personal interviews with
ery reader of this book. You will doubtless agree that
is would be impractical.

It *is* practical, however, to cover enough situations of
idespread application to point the way to successful
rsonality development for almost everybody, includ-
g you.

In later chapters we shall examine at length your rela-
onships with specific categories of persons and your own
anner of functioning in your various capacities as a so-
al and socializing human being. At this point, though,
e shall exploit our magical power as writer and reader
collaboration to peer unseen into the lives of people
aced by fate into situations in which, depending on
eir strengths or weaknesses, they can be lonely and un-
ppy, or happy and undeprived. We shall observe how
ne of them get along exceedingly well in circumstances

that might be devastating to others with less well-adjusted personalities; how others are lonely and miserable in situations that do not warrant such feelings; and how still others who at first are unable to cope with their problems finally manage to overcome them.

The purpose of this peeping and eavesdropping is to take you out of yourself for a brief period and give you a broad and philosophic view from on high. Though no two persons are exactly alike, there are in all the world no two persons who are altogether different from each other. If fingerprints vary in design, the number of fingerprints is the same for almost all. If one is emotional and the other phlegmatic, both can be happy and sad. If one is fat and the other thin, both are of flesh and blood. If one is educated and the other ignorant, both may be skillful. And so on.

Thus each of us can see in the personality of another some small reflection of himself; and even while we are examining the lives of others in a sort of detached way we can, and we doubtless shall, see in their problems and in their solutions some little thing that will be helpful to us in our own problems and solutions. Let us start with one who at first blush would seem to have in his life all of the elements that lead to bleak loneliness.

I know a lighthouse keeper, a bachelor, who sometimes goes for weeks without seeing or talking to a soul other than the man who once a week or so delivers his supplies. When I asked him whether he ever got lonely, he replied "Me lonely? Never! I've got books, I've got a radio, I get letters from my brother and from friends ashore, I've got my woodcarving hobby, and my memories of good and happy times in the past, and my anticipation of good things to come. The sea and the gulls and the wind and the stars are like friends and I love them all. I see my good friend Jim Hawkins, who brings me supplies, almost every week, and we have fine little chats about this and that. I see ships passing in the night and I feel good all over that my light lets the people in the ships sleep secure. Oh, sure, I figure that one of these days I'll give this up and go back and live with people again, but . . . do you know . . . I'm afraid that when I do, I'll miss all this."

My lighthouse keeper friend worries needlessly. A man like that will never be lonely.

On the other hand, I know a teacher who is constantly with people. She has students who admire and respect her and hold her in affection. She has friends who love her and are glad to be in her company. But almost always she feels that aching emptiness that we associate with loneliness.

It requires no psychoanalyst to get at the root of her problem. Her good friends know and understand what makes her so lonely, but though they try and try they seem unable to help. This teacher was once—still is—in love. Unfortunately, the man she loved transferred his affections to another woman and married her. These things happen every day and usually the deprived one, after a period of heartbreak, pulls out of it. In this case the teacher's misery, instead of abating with the passage of time, became something of a fixation. She can do nothing, see no one, without feeling in the back of her mind and in the depths of her heart an overwhelming sense of loss —of something missing—of emptiness that nothing and no one seem to be able to fill.

For her, and for others like her who suffer endless loneliness because of the loss of loved ones by death, or removal, or quarrel, there can be no release from loneliness through contact and association with people other than the ones for whom they yearn. They will be just as lonely in a crowded bus, at a birthday party, in a schoolroom, on an excursion or even, as may happen to some who make a desperate decision to do something about it, *at their own weddings*. Almost everyone knows someone who married on the rebound and wept inside throughout the wedding ceremony.

In such cases the conquest of loneliness *must come from within*. I am fully aware of the fact that it is one thing—a comparatively easy thing—to say to one who pines for a loved one, "You must take hold of yourself from within and stop your yearning"; and quite another thing—a most difficult thing—to act on the advice. And yet, in the absence of any patents in the Patent Office on genuinely magic devices, we poor human beings are left with the alternative of using the realistic, if comparatively ineffectual, devices available.

Indeed, the very first step toward the solution of any problem of the spirit, however small or great, is the acceptance of the fact that magic has not yet been invented, that miracles are of the distant past and the dim future, and that nowadays God helps them that help themselves while remaining willing to accept help from others.

The second step is the willingness and the ability to be brutal to one's self and to accept a sort of compassionate brutality at the hands of others. In the case of the teacher this would mean that she should sit down before her mirror and say, cruelly, to the image facing her: "It is over. He doesn't love you any more. He will never love you any more. He loves someone else who is now his wife. Your yearning for him is a form of mental adultery, a masochistic, perverted joy-pain, a cowardly withdrawal from reality. You are being unfair to those who do love you, for you are depriving them of a full measure of love in return; in a way you are doing a little bit to them what he did to you. It would not be unfair to you if they decided to withhold their love from you as you do from them; and you may expect that to happen, eventually, for they will not, like you, continue to love where love is not returned. Come out of that dream world, which is a hopeless blind alley, and come into the real world where the love of others, companionship, accomplishment and happiness are ready for you to grasp."

All this has been said far more concisely in the past: Accept inevitables. There is no alternative that leads anywhere but to unhappiness.

One caution must be uttered: before you accept it be sure it is an inevitable. The death of loved ones constitutes an inevitable. The apparent death of love does not.

For instance, the mere fact that a man says he is tired of a woman should not, of itself, lead the woman to accept it as an inevitable. The philosophy of the acceptance of inevitables must not be permitted to degenerate into a philosophy of a blind acceptance of the insolubility of any problem that arises. In the beginning, our teacher may have been justified in refusing to face the fact that her sweetheart no longer loved her. Perhaps by revising her approach to him, eliminating habits and attitudes that may have served to repel him, fighting the new love that came into his life, she might have won the day. In any event, the effort was one that should have been made by anyone with character and determination. It was only as time passed, and he became certain enough of his new love to marry her, that our teacher should have had the capacity for recognizing that the good fight had been lost —irretrievably. At that point, faced with an inevitable, it was necessary for her to make up her mind that she would go on living in the real world instead of withdrawing to the other.

If you are lonely because you have lost love or a loved one recently enough not to have it said of you that you have withdrawn more or less permanently into a state of yearning for what is no more, you will need the consolation of the company of others, of work, of new interests. In the pages ahead you may find hints and suggestions that will be helpful to you in finding this company, this work, these interests. Before all else, however, you must know and believe that for most mortals the wound heals with time. Even if you know it, you will find it desperately difficult to believe that it will be true in your case. Try to remember that other people have feelings and sorrows as deep as your own and that many of them have suffered more frequently than you have; and remember that the vast majority of them have recovered from their sorrow and have carried on with happiness restored. You are neither superior nor inferior to most other people and the chances are more than excellent that one day you, too, will wake to the morning with your sadness transformed into a loving memory that can be borne without weeping. When that morning dawns, your period of loneliness will be over. More, your suffering will have made you consciously kin to the others who have suffered. You will be a mellower, more understanding person than you ever were before, and you will be capable of a degree of friendship that will draw others to you to drive all chance of new loneliness away. Having known sorrow, you will have a greater capacity for happiness, for you will know happiness as more than a routine thing to be taken for granted. One who has starved savors food more than one who has known nothing but plenty.

A frequent indirect cause of loneliness is incompatibility. Take the case of Walter Taylor, mechanical engineer and husband of Miriam Taylor. He has been married to Miriam for fifteen years. He goes to work every weekday and comes home to Miriam every evening. He spends weekends with Miriam as he should, for she is his wife. It is plain to see that except for about forty hours a week he spends all of his time with his wife.

When he is at work or at lunch, he is not lonely. He has made friends at his office with men and women with whom he can talk and laugh and plan. He enjoys his work, and when he is not communing with his colleagues it absorbs him. For eight hours a day he is reasonably happy.

But when the clock strikes five his spirits begin to droop, for he is going home to Miriam. A sense of great loneliness pervades his soul and it lasts until he returns to the office the following morning. For he and Miriam are incompatible. She doesn't understand him at all. He can tell her only the most superficial things about his business life—that he has received a raise, that he is expected to work an extra hour tomorrow and will be home later than usual, that a fellow employee has become a father. Beyond the casual, bread-and-butter facts of life, Walter and Miriam find nothing to talk about. The silences last for hours, broken only by the drone of their television, which he watches with half a heart while his wife putters about her chores.

Walter and his wife are not incompatible in the sense that there is strife between them. If there were strife he might be unhappy but too busy fighting with her to be aware of loneliness. The incompatibility is the result of the fact that he is intelligent, idealistic, interested in world events and a dreamer, while she is stolid, matter-of-fact, dull. They have little in common and they have no children.

But Miriam is a good woman, as he is a good man. She is also a good wife, for she cooks his meals, mends his clothes, keeps his home orderly and does not squander his earnings. For him to leave her because he is lonely with her would be cruel, indecent and, in the eyes of the world, completely unjustified. The unhappiness of his loneliness is due to no conscious act on her part—she doesn't even know he is lonely, for he hasn't it in him to be cruel enough to tell her.

The world has millions of people who for similar or for vastly different reasons are living together with other people in loneliness. What are they to do short of casting out of their lives the people with whom they are lonely? How can they go on bearing the pain of loneliness without bursting out of their skins with the frustration of it? These are husbands and wives, brothers and sisters, parents and children. They are bound by ties of blood and law and the conventions, and separated by gulfs of misunderstanding of one another. What are they to do?

Well, you will recall that we said earlier that loneliness is the only emotion that cannot be shared. Does this constitute a contradiction? If sharing negates loneliness, how can people who are sharing their lives be lonely?

Actually, they can't be truly and completely lonely. Sometimes loneliness and self-pity become confused in the minds of men. Walter thinks he is lonely, and in a goodly measure he is lonely, because his wife does not meet him mentally. Instead of dwelling on the dull but vital things they have in common, he closes his mind to everything except what he is missing in a wife. Having taken this attitude, he is in no state to take any steps that might serve to increase the area of compatibility. All he can do is sigh and be sorry for himself because he feels lonely.

Now, the fact that sharing is a negation of loneliness does not mean that a little sharing will cure a big loneliness. That is why we must, in justice to Walter, admit the likelihood that his loneliness is not entirely self-pity any more than his self-pity is entirely loneliness. The crucial point is that where there is a foundation of sharing, no matter how limited, there is to that extent an absence of genuine loneliness and a possibility of building constructively on that foundation.

An interesting bit of proof that this is so in the case of Walter and Miriam came out one winter when she was ill and had to go to the country for a week to recuperate. Walter missed her. He didn't miss her desperately, but he missed her.

If Walter missed Miriam when she was away from him, he must have been more lonely without her than with her. Ergo, though he might have been less lonely living with someone else, he would have been more lonely living alone. The almost mathematical solution to this equation is this: rather than being the cause of his loneliness, Miriam was actually to some extent contributing to the lessening of his loneliness. Had Walter the wisdom and the insight to see this as the true picture of his life with Miriam, he might have gone on from there to the task of making it possible for her to do more and more each day to lighten his burden of loneliness.

You can accept that as an invariable rule no matter how black the picture may appear on the surface. When people live together, even in conditions of strife, they are to a greater or lesser extent making one another less lonely. If they are unable to build on that foundation a better, progressively less lonely life, it were better that they parted. But the breaking up of a family group must be undertaken only as a last, desperate resort.

If you are one of those who live in so-called incompatibility with others and are therefore too often lonely, do yourself a gigantic favor: step outside of yourself for a few moments and examine your situation objectively. Is the incompatibility partly your own fault, and if it is, don't you think you have more to gain than to lose by giving ground, perhaps swallowing some pride, than by carrying in your heart a resentment against the guilt of your cohabitants? Is your inability to find a common ground with your partner or partners perhaps the result of some measure of mental snobbishness, or jealousy, or impatience, or an overdemanding attitude on your part?

This goes for the bickering husbands and wives, the scrapping brothers and sisters, the harping parents and the irreverent children, to say nothing of the in-laws who must, because of economic necessity or some other act of fate, live together and do so in perpetual disharmony.

Maybe if you stopped seeing the mote in your husband's eye; maybe if you realized that your wife's preoccupation with the household instead of with the world news is quite excusable; maybe if you began to understand that the hateful things your brother or sister says or does are not really objectively hateful but become so to you because of some sibling resentment you are carrying; maybe if you came to understand that even though your parents are not as remarkably brilliant as you are they do nevertheless want you to be happy; maybe if you made up your mind that your children are not ingrates but are merely trying to make their way in their own way; maybe if you had some sympathy with the plight of the old folks who have to live with you; and maybe if you saw the viewpoint of the younger generation with whom you are compelled to live—why then, maybe, some of the incompatibility would begin to melt away, and with it, some of your loneliness.

It is obviously impossible to list in the space of one brief lifetime, and certainly in the space of one brief chapter, all of the millions of causes, real and apparent, of incompatibility; and so the reader will forgive me if the list above is woefully incomplete. The lesson to be learned is not dependent upon an exhaustive review of these reasons. Look at it this way: whatever may be the reasons for your living with the people with whom you live in such a manner as to make you miserable and lonely, there is no blinking the fact that you would be less lonely and less miserable if your relations with them were to take a turn for the better. From the purely selfish point of view you would profit from an earnest effort to find out wherein you may be contributing to the incompatibility and to take steps to reform where you see the need of reform. This would be profitable to you even if there were no reciprocal action, for even a unilateral improvement is an improvement.

However, human beings, if they are normal mentally, tend to respond in kind. If you are nasty, they will be nasty. If you are nice, they may still be nasty, but there will automatically be set up in them a conscience-pressure which at the worst will leave them less nasty than they would otherwise have been. It would be silly to tell you that if you went around radiating sweetness and light you would find everybody you met radiating sweetness and light in return. Indeed, if it were so, the world might be a rather insipid place in which to live. But it is not silly to tell you that if you radiate tolerance and kindness and understanding, you will at least find more sweetness and light around than if you do not.

And so, you may very well find that if you are caught in an incompatibility situation, a first step toward eliminating your own share in creating the situation will set up a chain reaction that could eventually eliminate, or at the very least considerably alleviate, the incompatibility and the resulting loneliness. You are more understanding, there is a tendency, as a result, to greater understanding on the part of your sparring partner; there is then an additional incentive to you to carry your understanding still further, and so on.

Nor need this approach be restricted to the sort of incompatibility associated with strife and disagreement. There was, for instance, no strife between Walter and Miriam. If Walter gave some thought to the fact that he was contributing to the incompatibility, he might come home one evening and show a little interest in Miriam's talk about her day's experiences with the butcher, the baker and the lady next door. He might even find it less dull than he expected. He might then try to tell her about some of the things that he had spoken about in the office that day. Certainly he would find her eager and receptive and perhaps, to his surprise, even capable of comprehending what he was saying. So much of his feeling of being alone when he is with her is, after all, a rationalization of a superiority feeling mingled with self-pity for the fact that one so interesting as he is compelled to live in wedlock with one so uninteresting as Miriam.

From there he could go on with a program of educating his wife in many little ways. He might offer her first some easy books for reading and discussion with him. He might take her out more to the theatre and to social evenings at the homes of friends. He might have friends in more often. He might bring her to the office and introduce her around and give her a visual picture of the place in which he is not lonely, so that when he spoke of it to her of an evening she would have, and he would feel that she had, a more intimate understanding. He could do a million and one things to pave the way to evenings of togetherness instead of loneliness if only he had the understanding that it was possible and the will to act on that understanding.

If you are the one who is lonely, you are the one who must make the first move. Don't let familiarity breed contempt. Don't get into a rut of prejudiced attitudes. Try to see the people with whom you live in a fresh light, as though you had never seen them before. You will find, almost all the time, that they are not as black as your mind has painted them and that you yourself are in some measure to blame for whatever incompatibility may exist, even if you are so perfect that your only fault is your failure to end the association. If you do not end the association, if you remain under the same roof, your only chance for happiness is to take the difficult but rewarding road from incompatibility and loneliness to compatibility and togetherness. To take that road you must walk on humble feet.

A third great cause of loneliness among people who are not physically alone is a by-product of the feeling that they are not wanted. This feeling of rejection may have any one of a number of causes: people grow old and begin to feel they are in the way; people become ill and are convinced that they are nothing but burdens to others; people are not pretty or handsome and imagine themselves therefore undesirable; people do not have the gift of gab and consider themselves too inadequate socially to be sought after; people are unsuccessful and cannot see how anybody would want to have anything to do with them; people are too tall or too short or too fat or too thin or too modest or too poor to be anything but zeros in the arithmetic of life.

If you are one of this vast army of rejects, discards, throwaways, and free samples, you must be lonely indeed, and only a cruel person like the present writer would have the hardness of heart to blame you for your misfortune. No decent person was ever rejected by the world. Not by the twentieth-century Western world at any rate. If you have been rejected, brothers and sisters, you have rejected yourselves.

Now please don't get me wrong. This is no inspirational attempt to disguise the facts of life. It is quite true that in our present stage of economic development, which lags about a hundred years behind the times in its psychological and humanitarian aspects, men and women who still have many years of productive capacity are deprived of opportunities to work in endeavors for which they are fully qualified. It is quite understandable that this refusal to take what they have to offer should come as a shock requiring complete reorientation.

It is also true that people who fall ill must add to the burdens of those about them; and that physically and socially handicapped people suffer a certain disadvantage in the game of love, or social exchange, or even friendship. If it were within our province in this volume to attempt a correction of economic attitudes or social concepts, we

REJECTED? BLAME YOURSELF 57

might go at this point into the causes and cures of whatever it is that ails our world. You will remember, however,
that we have agreed to limit ourselves to the problems of
loneliness in the hope that if we are able to solve these we
shall in some substantial measure ease the hurt that the
weaknesses of society inflict upon us.

The fact remains that multitudes of people who have
been hurt by nature or by society have managed by their
own thinking and attitudes to compensate in one way or
another to the degree that they live happy lives of togetherness with their fellows. If it be possible for one to
do this, it is possible for all within the limits of their own
capacities. That is to say, *it is not inherent in the nature of
things that these hurts must result in discard or loneliness.*

In fiction drawn from life there is a character that re-
curs frequently—the aged, bedridden aunt or mother or
father (and sometimes even an uncle or a cousin) who is
the center of group or family life—a person with such
strength of character, such interest in the lives of all, such
willingness to participate in these lives, that all of the
young and healthy and successful ones in the group are
dependent upon him in some measure. In such cases, from
inner causes alone, a person who might have been lonely
and convinced that he is an unwanted burden is actually
never lonely and demonstrably not unwanted.

Nobody who shows strength of character and an interest
in the lives of others is ever unwanted. Even people who
fail to show this strength or this interest are never unwanted to the degree that they must live a life of loneli-

ness. Nobody, in short, is discarded unless he first discards himself.

In the stock market it happens that certain traders in securities become convinced that the shares of a particular corporation are going to decrease in value. They then "sell short" the shares of that corporation. That is, they borrow shares from the stockbroker and sell them at current prices in the open market. If their calculations prove to be correct, they subsequently buy an equivalent number of shares at a lower price and return these shares to the broker from whom they borrowed the first shares. Their profit is the amount by which the shares have decreased in value since the day they were sold short.

Periodically there is published a report of the "short interest"—the number of shares borrowed and sold short —in various corporations. Other traders read these reports and are often guided in their transactions by the extent of the short interest. If the short interest in a certain company has increased considerably, they feel that "somebody knows something" and they, too, may feel inclined to sell short. In this way it is possible for a short interest to have a snowballing effect on the decrease in the price of the shares involved, regardless of the intrinsic worth of the shares.

The moral is: Never sell yourself short.

Selling yourself short is more damaging to you than selling stocks short is to the stocks. It is as though the president of a corporation himself were to sell short the shares of his own company. Who would know better than he whether short selling were justified? And who would know better than you whether your own value was on the way down?

This is a more serious matter than the absence of self-esteem, which we discussed earlier. In this we pass from a negative approach to your worth to a positive approach to your worthlessness. To put it another way, within the framework of our general thesis, you will experience more loneliness as a result of a conviction that you are nothing than out of your lack of conviction that you are something.

Are you nothing? Are you not worthy of the companionship of others? Is there any real reason for selling yourself short?

In a world of perfect, young, beautiful, healthy, brilliant, successful and confident people, an occasional oldster, invalid, failure or Milquetoast might be forgiven for having doubts about his place in the world. But look at the world. Add up the older people, the sick people, the unhandsome people, the unsuccessful people, the not-so-self-assured people, the far-from-brilliant people, and you will find that what is left is a minority and not such a large minority at that. Can it be that the great majority consists of people who deserve rejection? Or, from another point of view, can it be that the great majority consists of people who go through life rejecting the rest of the majority? Or, to place still another face on the matter, can it be that this great majority is dependent for acceptance upon that little band of perfect human beings comprising the small minority?

Isn't it obvious that it is silly and unrealistic to allow yourself to drift into the belief that you could be lonely and unwanted for any reason beyond your control? Isn't it mathematically demonstrable that if people were rejected for any of these reasons most of the people in the world would be rejected people? And isn't it perfectly evident that most of the people in the world are *not* rejected people?

You can take this for indisputable truth: if you do not sell yourself short, if you do not carry inside you the feeling that the world is rejecting you, the world will not reject you, and you will have friends and companions, and you will not be lonely. There is no need to point to the tens of thousands of plain girls who marry handsome husbands; the multitudes of old people who are revered, idolized and sought after by many friends; the countless unsuccessful or moderately successful people who have wonderful loves and friendships through their worst times; the many sick people who give others a sense of purpose and fulfillment because they are willing graciously to accept their help. These are all people who have refused to reject the world for fear the world was rejecting them; and so the world does not reject them.

When all the frills and superficialities are subtracted from human relationships the basic thing that one human being wants from another is devoted companionship.

There isn't a person in the world who cannot give this if he wants to.

Having said all this, I must confess that it will not be enough for you to make up your mind to give devoted companionship, or to believe that the world will not reject you. If you are already lonely because of any of the problems that have led you to feel lonely and rejected, you must start building anew. You can't just walk over to someone and say, "Now look here, I want to be your friend and I know you are going to like me." The kindest thing they would think of you if you did would be that you are a "little tetched in the haid."

At this juncture of our relationship as reader and writer we wish merely to establish the fact that none of the misfortunes, weaknesses or disabilities beyond your control are of themselves sufficient to cause you to be rejected. If you do feel rejected, you have only yourself to blame.

Chapter Four

A MILLION WAYS TO MEET NEW PEOPLE

❧ It is a strange commentary on our social mores that with the population of the earth increasing at an alarming rate; with highways and seaways and airways so crowded with trains and planes and cars and ships full of human beings that they move along engine to caboose, nose to tail, bumper to bumper and prow to stern; with schools and theatres and lecture halls and dance halls and concert halls and jails and parks and bars and apartment houses and churches and merry-go-rounds and stadiums and restaurants so jam-packed with people—it is a strange commentary that with all this abundance of God's children there are still so many of us who do not know how to find among them a few sympathetic souls whom we can draw to our bosoms and say: "Let's be friends together, let's commune together, let's exchange thoughts and fears and aspirations and dreams and joys and sorrows."

Strange though it be, the fact remains that thousands upon thousands of us move about in the world encased in personal iron curtains that keep us lonesomely imprisoned within and our fellow human beings indifferently, even unknowingly, exiled to the wide outside.

I am periodically moved to pity by the plaintive cry: "I don't know how to meet people. Oh, I have my family and maybe a friend or two, but I want romance, variety, adventure, excitement. I want to spread out. I want to exchange ideas with new people. I can't just walk up to a stranger and say, 'See here, I'd like to know you.' I can't just pick people out of a crowd and get chummy with them. I want to expand my horizons—I want to grow outward—but how? How can I get to know new people?"

Well, I have figured it out on my computer and I find that there are precisely one million and sixty-three ways to get to know new people. I don't mean just getting introduced to them so you know their names and little more; I mean really getting to know them as intimately as you may wish. This poses a problem. The publisher of this volume adamantly refuses to provide sufficient pages to list the entire one million and sixty-three methods. Indeed, there is some question whether we can even find the space for the odd sixty-three methods without infringing on important chapters still to come. The problem is: How can we see to it that you get some benefit out of the findings of my computer? The only way out of the dilemma is the employment of a formula. Once you have a formula for the solution of a problem, you can, with the formula, solve all problems of the same kind. Thus, if we can arrive at a formula for meeting people on Main Street or in a factory, we can use the formula for meeting people on Jay Street or in a school. Anyone, then, who becomes proficient in the use of the formula will be able to find for himself the entire one million and sixty-three ways of meeting new people.

Fortunately, though the formula is so little known as to be almost a secret formula, I have been able to ferret it out and in a moment or two I shall reveal it to you.

First, however, I want to assure you that you will not find in these pages any suggestion that you adopt the old methods that continue to be tried though they have long been found wanting. You are not going to be advised to take courses in a night school, or to go to dances, or to join a social club, or to take a tour or a cruise with a travel group. It may be possible to make friends by doing these things, but many people walk home alone from night school and remain wallflowers or stag-line habitués at dances, silent and unnoticed members of social clubs and forgotten participants in group tours and cruises.

The art of making friends or at least cordial acquaintances out of strangers lies not in going to places where strangers congregate but rather in getting people involved in something with you as an individual rather than you as a member of a group. It is the involvement that counts, not the mere contact; it is your centrality in an activity or a situation rather than the activity or the situation itself that matters.

And there you have the secret.

Let's take one of the discarded methods mentioned above and see how the formula works. Mary is lonely and blue and her mother, full of pity, says: "Mary, why don't you join a social club and meet some new people?"

Deciding she has nothing to lose, Mary takes her mother's advice. She joins the Midville Social Club, dues three dollars a year. She attends all meetings, strikes up a nodding, even a speaking, acquaintance with a few people. She participates in some measure in the various discussions that come up at membership meetings. For a few weeks she begins to think that maybe her mother was right.

But people are people, and Mary is Mary, and soon she finds that she has come up against her own iron curtain and some other little curtains containing cliques and old friends to whom Mary is a newcomer and an outsider, even though she is a fully paid-up member. No handsome, dashing swain finds her so alluring that he must sweep her off her feet. No friendly, sympathetic girl sees in Mary the true friend for whom she has always sought. And pretty soon the only difference in Mary's life is that now she belongs to a social club. Her loneliness, which for a while had been mitigated by new contacts, now sweeps back into her soul with added intensity.

That is the picture of Mary when she tried to meet people merely by going to places where people were and hoping that something would happen to cause some of these people to become an important part of her life.

Why, except by some accident of fate or by some stroke of luck, should any of the other members of the club change the established pattern of their lives and friendships by opening the gates to Mary? Why should they especially notice Mary at all? Mary isn't brilliant, she isn't ravishingly beautiful, she has no great talents. She is just another nice girl in a world full of nice girls.

But now let us see what happens when Mary discovers our formula . . . even when she uses it in such an outworn approach as joining a social club.

One evening Mary attends the regular monthly business meeting of the club. It starts out like any other evening and like any other meeting. The minutes are read. Reports on ticket sales for the forthcoming dance are rendered by the committee. A slate of officers for the next election is presented to the members. The treasurer reads the financial report. Then the club chairman opens the meeting to statements on "Good and Welfare."

Grace rises to say that she thinks it would be a good idea for the club to have a picnic next summer. Henry says that some of the boys ought to get together to repaint the clubroom. Then Mary asks for the floor and is recognized by the chairman.

Mary, her heart in her mouth, rises and says: "I know that lots of our members have cameras and I know how much it costs to have enlargements made of some of your favorite pictures. My father has a darkroom in our house and he's taught me to make enlargements. If any of the members want to use our darkroom, I'll be glad to show them how it's done and they can make their own enlargements without any expense except the cost of the paper."

Now this was no general statement about a general matter that affected everyone in the club in a general way. It was a statement that put Mary right in the middle of it. It made Mary the center of an operation. No one could participate in the operation without thinking first of all and last of all about Mary as an individual, as the individual upon whom the operation rested.

There was no flurry of excitement when Mary had said her nervous little piece. The meeting proceeded along the even tenor of its way until the moment of adjournment. After the meeting, however, two of the boys and one of the girls came over to Mary to discuss her proposal with her. The four of them arranged for a meeting at Mary's home at which she would show them how to make enlargements from their negatives.

What was the result? For a few weeks the quartet worked with feverish enthusiasm at the new hobby. Gradually, however, their ardor for enlargements began to cool and the darkroom sessions became a rarity. But in the meantime the girl and one of the boys found in Mary, through frequent association, a kindred soul. She was no more kindred now than she had been before she launched her enlargement program, but because she had been so positively the center of the project the others inevitably had to give her special thought and attention—partly from a feeling of gratitude for her help, partly because they were, in a sense, her pupils. As their teacher she was in what might be called an exalted position *vis-à-vis* the others. And so they discovered what they might never have discovered had she not made herself the center of an operation. They discovered that Mary was the kind of girl they liked. Thus Mary made two good friends.

There is an interesting thing about our formula: while, at times, it may call for certain special knowledge or ability that may easily be acquired, it does not call for any great charm or talent or extroversion, though it may serve to help develop all three in those who make use of it. In addition, as we shall see, the formula can serve to make not only friends, but money as well.

I know an elderly woman who lives alone in an old house in which her family, of which she is the only survivor, had lived for generations. She is a shy person, sweet and lovable, but almost tongue-tied in the presence of strangers. For several years after the death of her husband there were no visitors at her home other than the mailman, the laundry boy and such other servicemen as she needed for the running of her household. She was, as I learned later, terribly lonely during these years.

The neighbors were sorry for her but since she invited no association they granted her the privacy they thought she wanted. I myself used to pass by her home every day. Sometimes she would be seated by the window and we would nod to each other. One day, as I passed, I saw her

slumped over the sill as though asleep. When I had proceeded about half a block I was filled with a sudden un-
easiness. People didn't look just like that when they were
asleep. I hurried back and found her still motionless, in
the same position. I called to her but she did not answer
or move. I rushed to the door which, fortunately, was
unlocked and entered the house. When I got to her I
found that she was not dead, as I had feared, but burning
with fever. I got her onto the sofa and telephoned a doctor.

While I awaited his arrival I looked about the room. It
was crammed full of furniture, lamps, vases, clocks and
doodads, some of which appeared even to my unpracticed
eye to be valuable antiques. I recall that I wondered why
this old lady held on to such a jumble of stuff, so little of
which could be of use to her.

The doctor arrived and diagnosed her illness as in-
fluenza. He was kind enough to say to her that I might
have saved her life by calling him when I did. When I
left, one of the neighbors, whose curiosity had been
aroused by the arrival of the doctor, asked me what was
wrong. When I told her, she said that she would get a
group of the women in the neighborhood together to take
turns in caring for their sick neighbor.

Though it is not the point of the story, it is interesting
to note that in an unhappy sort of way the old lady was
now the center of an operation, the focus of attention, and
as such she was about to be given the opportunity of making a number of friends in the neighborhood.

When she recovered, the old lady invited me in one day as I was passing by. She wanted to thank me for what I had done. We got to talking and she told me, in response to a question, that since she did not have much money she had tried to sell some of her treasures to a secondhand-furniture dealer. However, he had offered her such a pittance that she had decided not to sell anything.

I induced her to invest a few of her dollars in an advertisement in a neighborhood newspaper. In this ad she was to mention only one of the items she possessed and she was to speak of it as a prized possession with which she was reluctant to part, which was true. A high price was to be placed on the object but the price was not to be greater than its real worth. Anyone who knew about such things and had the money and the desire to own one would prove a live prospect.

I had no thought at the time of helping her to solve her loneliness problem. The idea then was to get her some money for her needs. Well, we got both the money and the loneliness cure.

There were three applicants for the item which had been offered. One was a woman who made a specialty of finding such things and reselling them, one was a man who lived, breathed and dreamed antiques, and the third was a newly wed bride who was setting up her home and who had been attracted by the advertised description. My friend sold it to the bride for reasons which you can understand; but all three were charmed by her and her home and all three became friends and frequent visitors.

The woman with the business angle saw in the old woman's home a treasure trove of business possibilities. More intriguing to her than the items themselves was the setting in this private old home. She worked out an arrangement whereby many of the items would be sold and replaced with others. In short, she went into business with my friend, using her home as the bait—a quite legitimate bait.

The man who loved antiques bought two other items and got to like the old lady so well that he began to make it a practice to drop in for tea even when he was not particularly concerned with antiques. The bride, too, began to make periodic visits.

Beyond these, there were new customers each week, all of them conscious of the fact that they were visiting a private home. This made them more conscious of the old lady as an individual than they might have been had they been shopping in a store. Many of them were quite willing to become friendly and after a while the old woman's problem changed from loneliness to the need for finding time for privacy and communion, a much more pleasant problem indeed. Need I add that there was quite an improvement in the money situation as well?

I have told this story at length because it illustrates so well the value of our formula—the importance of being the center of the operation, the possibility of utilizing things already a part of our lives in the effort to get beyond the present boundaries of our lives, even though we may not be rich or beautiful, or talented, or aggressive, or extrovert, or articulate. It illustrates one thing more, and this is the other side of the coin on which our formula is engraved: the utter willingness of people to enter into our lives once their interest in us is aroused. The making of new friends is not a battle; it is a simple technique that anyone can employ. If you understand this it is fair to say that loneliness resulting from lack of human contacts need never again be your lot.

Well, then, you have the formula and you have had two illustrations of the operation of the formula. As I have indicated, this should be sufficient to enable you to figure out the balance of the one million and sixty-three ways of making new friends. However, before going on to the next phase of our main theme we may, with profit, list ten or twenty additional ways of bringing new people inside your private iron curtain, leaving only a trifle over a million for you to find by yourself.

The techniques that follow are not new, though most of them will probably be new to you. They have been culled from a lifetime of observation in many fields. In most cases those who followed these techniques did not do so for the purpose of curing loneliness; rather they were interested in the activities themselves or they were ambitious for public acclaim or they wanted to make money or they just happened to do the things they did because that's the way the cards were dealt.

Nevertheless, an inevitable by-product in every case was a broadening of the horizons of friendship. For you, this by-product will be the main product and the other benefits will be by-products.

1. We have already observed that the act of sharing is incompatible with loneliness. What, therefore, could be a more fitting technique to head our list than one whose very essence is sharing? It is a matter of cosmic justice that one of the best areas of human endeavor in which to make friends is in the area of organized charity.

    Let me hasten to add that one does not, in this field, make friends of the recipients of charity. The Hebrew Talmud, to which I have referred once before, points out that "true charity is practiced in secret. The best type of almsgiving is where a person gives a donation without knowing who receives it, and a person receives it without knowing who donated it." This lack of contact between giver and receiver is perhaps the greatest merit of organized charity.

    Organized philanthropies and public service causes such as those which fight the killer diseases are always wide open and grateful for volunteer workers as well as for donors. I know scores of men and women who have made prized and lasting friendships through work on committees of such organizations. All that is required is a willingness to serve in any of a score of ways. You may make your home available for a meeting of prospective donors. If you have an interesting collection of unusual or rare items such as stamps, or costumes, or furniture, or ship models, etc., you may make it available as a focus for a fund-raising project. You may be willing to accept the chairmanship of a committee. Activities such as these are calculated to conform with our formula in that they make you the center of the operation. However, there are also group activities which are, in this particular field, almost as good for your purpose. For instance, you may agree to sell raffle tickets or dance tickets for a worthy cause. You may be a part of a volunteer group for addressing envelopes and making telephone calls. You may undertake to solicit contributions from house to house.

If you continue for an extended period of time to dedicate yourself to such work in your spare hours, you will eventually become associated in the minds of all the members of your community with the particular cause for which you are working. To these people you will appear to be—even if you are only a cog in a committee or a group—the center of an operation.

Whatever may be your role you will find yourself in collaboration with people who are a cut above average, for it takes exceptional people to sacrifice the time and energy required for such service. What is more, you will be a part of a group which is imbued with the fervor of doing good and with the satisfaction that comes of doing good. This fervor and this satisfaction make for a camaraderie in which friendships blossom easily.

And it's the easiest thing in the world. All you you have to do is to select a cause in which you feel you can be sincerely interested, telephone its local office and say: "I want to help." From that moment on you will be carried along the tide of some interesting events, away from the shore of loneliness toward the banks of togetherness.

2. Another activity in which service to the community is a basic factor is political activity. I do not mean the sort of political activity that will result in your becoming Governor or County Dog Catcher; if you need help in meeting new people you are presumably not so outgoing that you can do the speechifying and handshaking and baby-kissing and all of the other acts of extroversion implicit in a political campaign in your own behalf. (Which is not to say that once you get your feet wet such a possibility is out of the question. There is one Assemblyman in a major eastern city who never dreamed, when he rang doorbells in a campaign to get out the vote, that one day he would be asking for votes for himself.)

There are in most communities civic and voters' associations which have as their aims the improvement of the communities and education in citizenship. They battle for new playgrounds, for noise abatement, to get people to register and to vote, to cure juvenile delinquency, for more policemen, for reform in government, and many other worthwhile goals.

If you have studied these movements, you know that while all right-minded citizens are in accord with their purposes, they have the darnedest time getting people actively involved in the task of actually working for these purposes. Everybody seems to say, "I'd like to see that done, but let George do it."

My advice to you is to be George, and do it. If the slackers and the shirkers knew what joys of accomplishment they are missing, what companionship and association they are allowing to slip through their fingers, they'd rush to their telephones to enlist. Be smart. Join up. It's as easy as becoming involved in philanthropic work and the rewards are exactly the same.

3. It isn't necessary to be noble to make friends, though it's a good idea to combine the effort with nobility if you can manage it. Some of the techniques to follow lack the touch of altruism and high purpose which we have noted in philanthropy and political activity, but they do provide ways of meeting new people.

Take dogs, for instance. Millions of lonely people have used their faithful cockers and bulls and Pekingese and collies and Dalmatians and dachshunds and just plain mutts as decoys for meeting new people.

If you haven't discovered the joys of dog ownership—if you haven't learned that when you take a cute little mongrel down the street he can make twenty acquaintances for you for every block you walk—do make it your business to give a home to a yearning canine and watch him go to work for you. Even if dogs didn't have this talent for making friends they'd take a little off the edge of your loneliness by their very nearness and by their love for you. But they *do* have the great talent, so why not make use of it?

4. Do you own a share of American industry? Stocks and bonds can be as companionable in your lonely hours as money in the bank. You remember how happy King Midas was with his many friendly gold pieces before he became a little too greedy.

Here's a little gimmick you can employ when you tire of counting your own gold pieces. Go to a stockbroker and ask him to buy you some shares in a sound American corporation that holds its quarterly or annual meetings in or near your city. Whether you buy one share or a thousand you immediately become a voting member of the corporation. You are privileged to attend its meetings and to participate in deliberations on major questions affecting the business and yourself as a stockholder.

In most instances you will be warmly welcomed at the meetings. Currently there is a vogue among the larger corporations for making the meetings of their stockholders festive occasions. Lunches or dinners or snacks are served, plant tours are arranged, expository movies are shown, souvenirs are distributed and a sort of club atmosphere prevails.

There is no greater community of interests than the community of financial interest among people who hardly know one another personally. When you attend a stockholders' meeting you may be certain that everyone else who is there is vitally interested in anything you may have to say that affects the corporation. You are considered a partner in a business in which everyone present has a share.

If you study the reports of your corporation as they are mailed to you, and if you come to intelligent conclusions about decisions that will benefit the corporation, you may even become competent to comment at meetings about the plans of the corporation. Such comment will make you the center of an operation for a little while and people are almost certain to approach you later to compliment you or to disagree with you. In either event, you will be given the opportunity to get to know them better.

If you attend the stockholders' meetings regularly, you will eventually find yourself being greeted by other regulars as an old friend, which will mean that you really *are* an old friend.

And remember, for very little money you can be a shareholder in a number of corporations because, as I have said, you need buy only one share. If you really want to extract maximum value from this technique, you might shop among stockholders at the meetings of numerous corporations until you find a group that suits your fancy best.

5. If you have something you don't need, and need something you don't have, place a little ad in the paper offering to swap. You can meet more people that way! There is a regular cult of swappers in the United States—people who always seem to need what someone else no longer wants. I suspect that many of them do their swapping because it helps them to meet so many interesting people. But what's wrong with that?

6. Do you live alone? We'll have a whole chapter about that later. In the meantime, just a word. If you share your apartment or house with someone who needs to share, you won't be living alone any more. Or had you already thought of that?

7. Mrs. Eldridge has a dozen new friends who love her, who are grateful to her and who pay her.

Mrs. Eldridge charges twenty dollars to run birthday and other parties for kiddies if the parents buy the food and the decorations; fifty dollars, more or less (depending on the number of children), if they don't.

The parents are delighted to be relieved of the bother of decorating the house for the party, preparing the goodies, keeping order, planning games and activities and seeing that the guest kiddies enjoy themselves.

Said one of the mothers (these mothers are wives of fairly successful businessmen and executives, of course): "Mrs. Eldridge is worth her weight in gold."

You too can be worth your weight in gold. This is an interesting activity and it does make you very much the center of an operation.

8. Henry Wilderling writes letters to the newspapers. They are not crank letters. They are just letters which express his opinions on various matters that interest him. Sometimes something he writes inspires a reader to write to him. Sometimes a regular correspondence starts. Sometimes this leads to a meeting and a friendship. If you can write letters, you can write letters to editors. And maybe something you write will do some good and, at the same time, make a friend for you.

9. What you do to get what you want often depends on how badly you want what you want. People move mountains to get the diamonds out of them. Other people forego delicious viands in order to remain slim. Some women spend tedious and un-

comfortable hours in beauty shops to enhance their attractiveness. Some people risk their lives in an automobile to get from one place to another five minutes sooner. How far are you willing to go to make friends?

Are you, perhaps, ready to move to another town? In an earlier chapter we agreed that it is possible to be lonely in a crowded place—in the heart of a big city, for instance. If you are one of the lonely ones who live in a big city you might be delightfully surprised at the change which a move to a small town might make in your life.

I remember that when I lived in a small town one of the most interesting things to my friends and me was the moving in of a new family. For days, and sometimes weeks, the newcomers were the subject of special attention, very much the center of the operation. Old-timers, one after another, visited and offered to be of assistance. Invitations to dinner and to membership in local organizations poured in. The only problem for the newcomers was how to place a limit on the time they had to give to the old-timers who could easily become friends with a little encouragement.

Moving from a city to a small town just to over-come loneliness and meet new people is a drastic, often inconvenient, usually impractical step. But then, it depends on how badly you want what you want.

10. There is always the danger of anonymity in numbers. That is the whole point of the "center of the operation" formula. The smaller the group in which you operate, the easier it is to be the center of the operation. If the group is small enough, it isn't even necessary to be the center of the operation to receive the desired degree of attention.

Another one of the things you were promised is that I would not advise you to do anything as ordinary as going to a night school for the purpose of meeting new people. I pointed out the limitations of this approach.

On the other hand, if you are going to take courses in a night school in any event you can improve your chances of success by selecting your courses with an eye to your purpose, which is to meet new people.

In selecting your courses remember the danger of anonymity in numbers. Pick subjects which attract the smallest number of students. A friend of mine, whom we shall call Jack Spenciling, told me he once attended a music harmony class in which there were only four students besides himself. One of them eventually became his partner in business, one became a customer of the business and one became his wife. I asked him what happened to the fourth student. "He married my sister," said Jack.

11. In the same way, a flautist might be more successful at a party than a pianist. Everybody and his

mother plays the piano. How many people do you know who play the flute?

One of the more delightful ways of meeting new people is through participation in musical endeavor. If you study music, study an instrument that will give you the best opportunity to participate in group music. (Music groups are usually so small that you don't have to bother about the center-of-the-operation formula. Every instrument in a quintet is the center of an operation.) Since there are so many violinists and pianists and drummers, try one of the other instruments. I have known any number of amateur orchestra leaders who searched every nook and cranny in town for harpists and oboe players while piano players couldn't even get interviews with them.

Please don't get me wrong. I love the piano and it's the only instrument I play. But nobody ever asks me to play.

12. Some morning, when you wake up in a lonely world and you sigh and you wish you knew how to go about meeting new people, just start something in your neighborhood.

Get up a petition for a new playground, for instance, and ask the neighbors to sign. Or send out letters asking everyone to chip in for the construction of a neighborhood swimming pool. Or organize a civic group. Or establish a cooperative venture like hiring a man to clear everybody's leaves away, or do everybody's plumbing or sit with everybody's kids. Or organize a picnic or a theatre party. In other words, just start something.

Anything like this makes you the center of the operation with a vengeance. And you'll be able to take your pick of new friends before many days of activity have passed. It bears repeating: Everybody agrees that useful things should be done but they expect George to do them. Then, when George does do them, George becomes a sort of VIP in their eyes and they look up to him, they like to talk to him, they offer him advice, they invite him to their homes, and they buy him gifts—anything to keep George doing it.

Again—be George. Do it. You'll love doing it and you'll make lots of friends.

13. Old Mrs. Warren has friends all over the world because on her lawn she keeps, of all things, one of the first automobiles manufactured in the United States. People come for miles to see it. Foreigners visiting her town consider a visit to Mrs. Warren's lawn a must, like the Eiffel Tower, or the Golden Gate Bridge, or the Catacombs.

The car got onto the lawn by accident. It was moved there when the barn in which it had been kept was being torn down to make room for an extension to her home. So many people came and admired it and spoke to Mrs. Warren about it that she got to like the idea and just left it there. News of the ancient car spread by word of mouth and soon it made Mrs. Warren the center of an operation that might literally be called worldwide. Certainly she never lacked for acquaintances.

Doesn't this give you some ideas? Mightn't you buy something extremely unusual or something of historic interest and let the word get around that you have it? You needn't put it on your lawn (though what would be wrong with that?) but you could keep it where people who were interested might get to it. And to you.

14. Can you fix toys? It's easy. Any grown-up can fix simple toys, the fixing of which seems too difficult to a child. Let the word get around among the kids that you fix toys as a hobby. Kids are funny. They'll even break toys on purpose to get you to fix them, so you needn't worry about attracting customers. Soon you'll get to know the kids, and when you know kids you get to know their parents or their older brothers and sisters. It never fails.

If you want to branch out, you can organize a toy exchange center in your home in which kids who are tired of the toys they have can meet kids who are also tired of their toys. This is a wonderful service for children and will warm the cockles of your heart even if it never makes you a grown-up friend. But it *will* make you grown-up friends, for you must never agree to an exchange until both children have letters of approval from their mothers or fathers addressed to you. Get it?

15. People are needed in Civil Defense. Get into it. You'll be performing a patriotic duty and at the same time will become a member of a select group of citizens tied together by a common bond of service—a group of Georges who do it while others shirk. Many of them will become your friends.

16. If you read a book or an article or a story and like it, write the author and tell him so. Address him or her through the office of the publisher or the magazine office. Writers are almost human and they like a kind word now and then. Some of them are really awfully nice and they'll write back. I know, because I've made friends of half a dozen people who wrote to me about something I had had published. One of them even wrote to tell me he didn't like one of my articles and when I replied that I didn't like it either, he said I didn't know what I was talking about and that he had been mistaken in his original criticism. We got quite chummy after that. This method doesn't make for mass friendships but you do often get to meet some really interesting people.

17. Everybody wants something for nothing. If you will offer a prize for the best recipe for cheese cake or for the first solution to a puzzle or for anything else that ordinary people can do, lots of ordinary people

will try to win the prize. And you will become the center of the operation, which means your horizons of acquaintanceship will be widened. All you have to do is to send a publicity release to your local newspaper. (Don't try this on a metropolitan newspaper.)

18. If you have a car, and if you are shy about making friends with your neighbors, and if you know some of them by sight, and if they wait for buses to the railroad station in the morning, you might just by chance drive along the bus route some mornings and invite a few of them to come along with you. There is no one more grateful than the person who gets a lift in the early morning, and no one more eager to talk and to be friendly.

If you want some benefit out of this beyond the cure of loneliness, you might do your shopping on the return trip.

If your loneliness is the sort that is brought on by paucity of human contacts, the formula you have been given and the examples of the way in which the formula works which have been presented should be sufficient to end your loneliness for all time. (Of course, if this is not the only contributing factor, you have more reading to do.)

Don't forget the formula. If you have ever seen what happens to a nobody who gets a part in a play or a bore who gets to make a speech to an audience or a simpleton who is elected to public office, you will understand its validity. People who wouldn't ordinarily deign to greet them will practically ask for their autographs. It's a funny world and you can't laugh in it until you realize how funny it is.

Chapter Five

MAKE YOURSELF COLORFUL

❧ In the preceding chapter we referred to the huge numbers of people who travel about the world, bumper to bumper, so to speak. This is now referred to as the population explosion. Scientists are concerned that there may soon be too many people in the world. There are already three billion, in spite of several major wars and a shocking increase in automobile fatalities. You would think, wouldn't you, that it might be pretty difficult for you to stand out in a crowd like that.

Actually it would not be at all difficult. All you need is the desire to stand out and the willingness to learn how. The reason for this is not that you are so wonderful but that of the three billion people now alive, about two billion, nine hundred and ninety-nine million will spend their time conforming and trying to be as alike as peas in a pod. They will be eager to dress and look alike, and to read and do and say the same things. That leaves the field wide open for you and the other nine hundred ninety-nine thousand, nine hundred and ninety-nine who don't think that successful living means disappearing into the general mass of humanity.

Of the million who want to be different, there are perhaps ten or at most twenty thousand who will be colorful or outstanding in a big way. These will be the presidents, the kings and queens, the members of congresses and parliaments, the stage and movie stars, the famous authors, the great musicians, the grande dames of society, the brilliant scientists, the talented artists, the notable doctors and lawyers and the like. You and I can hardly aspire to join this select group, though you never can tell.

Then there are the nine hundred and eighty or ninety thousand who will be outstanding in a smaller way—in their own towns or streets or offices or schools or clubs or homes. These are the colorful little people of the world: the people without whom no party is a success; the people who attract friends as though by magnet; the people with whom members of the opposite sex easily fall in love; the people who light up a room when they enter it.

You can be one of them if you want to be; and if you join this highly restricted club of nine hundred and eighty or ninety thousand colorful souls you will never be lonely again.

Paradoxically, you don't have to be outstanding to be outstanding. That is to say, it is not necessary to be handsome or beautiful or exceedingly clever or talented. How many times have you attended weddings at which you murmured, "I don't see what that gorgeous female sees in that ugly brute," or "How in the world did that frump ever get an Adonis like that to propose to her?" It happens too often to be explained away with the old saw that love is blind. As a matter of fact, love is not blind. Love comes as the result of true 20/20 vision. The chances are that the frump and the ugly brute have something that transcends mere surface appearance—something that arouses the interest and sharpens the vision of the Adonis and the gorgeous female.

Let me tell you about a "frump" who married not one Adonis, but two. (Not at the same time, of course. She divorced the first one because he turned out to be too colorful in his own right.) I shall have to disguise the details a bit, because I would not want her to recognize herself and hate me for it. No woman likes to be referred to as a frump.

The first thing to tell is that Lorna (let us call her that) never thought of herself as a frump. She knew she wasn't pretty, or talented, or even exceedingly smart, but she knew also that she was a human being, a woman, a creature capable of dignity and self-respect. She knew that she had something precious to give to the world, even if it were only love, or kindness, or companionship. Finally, she knew that what she had to give to the world could be given by the whole three billion human beings and that in order to get the world to accept her gifts she would have to do something that would make her noticed in that huge mass.

I don't think she sat down consciously and thought it out and planned it that way, though you can do it consciously if you wish. It just happened to occur to her because she was not satisfied just to have friends or to find a husband. She wanted the friends of her choice and the husband of her dreams. Almost everybody has friends and almost everyone finds a spouse, but most people take what they get or, at most, they make compromises.

It was quite by accident that she discovered that the most important ingredient of color in the human personality is enthusiasm. Without enthusiasm no human being can be outstanding or colorful or even talented. Can you imagine a half-hearted recital by an Artur Rubenstein, or an uninterested campaign speech by a Presidential aspirant, or an absent-minded proposal of marriage by a Romeo?

It happened like this. One day Lorna was shopping in a department store. On a novelty counter she came upon a little ivory elephant that struck her fancy. The more she looked at it, the more she admired it and soon, though it cost more than she should have spent, she felt that she could not do without it. She took it home and put it on a mantel where everyone who visited her could see it. She told her friends about it in such an enthusiastic way that some who had never called at her home asked if they could come and see it. After a while, the ivory elephant incident, like all world-shaking incidents, petered out and that would have been the end of it except for a lucky accident.

One of her office associates happened to vacation in Argentina. One day, in a shop window in Buenos Aires, she saw a number of carved ivory elephants of various sizes that had been imported from Siam, now Thailand. Suddenly she remembered how excited Lorna had been about her ivory elephant. This will make a wonderful gift for Lorna, she thought. She imagined how Lorna would bubble over when she received it and she felt good all over because she was going to bring such pleasure to her office friend. Of all the things she bought on her vacation for family and friends, the one that stood out in her mind was the elephant because this was the only one she knew for certain would be eagerly received.

She was not disappointed. Lorna's eyes lighted up so that the donor tingled all over. Forever after, there would be something about Lorna that made her very special in her own heart, even if later on she would forget the real reason for it. Naturally, she told others about Lorna's enthusiasm. "Lorna's just a nut about ivory elephants," she said, and soon Lorna came to be known as the elephant girl to her friends. They began to vie with one another to find odd and unusual ivory elephants to take to Lorna.

Lorna had become colorful! As simply as that!

The lesson was not lost on Lorna. She knew it was not the elephants *per se* that had almost suddenly changed her personality. It was her *enthusiasm* for the elephants that had the magnetic effect on the others. Indeed, when the first Adonis fell in love with her he didn't even know about the elephants. He became drawn to her because she was so much fun to be with; and she was so much fun to be with because she was enthusiastic. She didn't merely accept things; she clearly appreciated and enjoyed them, whether they were clever comments, a bright moon, a thoughtful gift or a friend's good fortune.

When he found out about the elephants, Mr. Adonis was delighted, because it gave him unending opportunities for surprising and delighting Lorna. In a sense, most of us are pretty wonderful people, because we get so much joy out of the ability to give joy. The hidden secret in this quality is the fact that one of the greatest joys we can give to others is *the easy opportunity to give us joy.* The reason is that our egos are flattered when we find ourselves capable of arousing enthusiasm in others.

You will note that in Lorna's case there were two factors that contributed to her achievement of colorfulness. One was the basic, fundamental, vital factor of enthusiasm, which was, and became more emphatically, an integral part of her personality. The second was her special interest in carved ivory elephants, which was not so basic or fundamental, but which was, in a way, almost as important. This second factor we shall call a gimmick, because that's what it was—a gimmick.

As we proceed, we shall see that what the basic personality factors accomplish for us is good, but not quite as good as what we could have with the addition of a gimmick. It is the basic personality factor that makes us likable and desirable, but it is the gimmick that makes it

easier for others either to please us (and therefore themselves) or place us in a mental compartment separate from
that reserved for the mass of faceless people. (When Lorna
married her second Adonis she was considerably older,
and the second time the ivory elephants played a bigger
role.)

Many of the outstanding people we discussed earlier—
the outstanding group of ten or twenty thousand who
come to wide public notice—consciously or instinctively
utilize the gimmick in addition to their basic talents or personality superiorities. A number come easily to mind.
Franklin Delano Roosevelt was one of our great Presidents
and he would find his place in history without a gimmick.
Nevertheless most of us, when we think of him, picture in
our minds at once the long, long cigarette holder with
the cigarette pointing almost skyward. The image of the
irascible Mayor who once headed the government of New
York City always includes the big ten-gallon hat. Indeed,
when the play *Fiorello* was produced, the big hat was an
indispensable prop. Winston Churchill played up the "V"
for victory sign with his fingers and still retained the
original gimmick of the big cigar which he chewed, rather
than smoked. President Kennedy affected a rocking chair;
President Eisenhower made use of the name "Ike"; President Truman played up the early-morning walk; Jack
Benny employed the gimmick of stinginess; Ted Lewis
wore a stovepipe hat; Kate Smith became the Moon over
the Mountain girl; you can add to the list for hours.

Before we go on it is necessary to sound a note of caution. I wouldn't want anyone, on the strength of what I have written thus far, to rush out and acquire a gimmick. The wrong gimmick could make things worse for you, rather than better. There is a fine line between being colorful and being a freak. *The gimmick has to be made to order for you.*

To illustrate the point, we might take some of the gimmicks mentioned above and transpose them. If President Roosevelt had worn La Guardia's ten-gallon hat, the gimmick would have made him a freak. Roosevelt was not the big-hat type. If President Kennedy were to chew Churchillian cigars he would appear ridiculous. If Eisenhower had pretended to be stingy, the gimmick would have been plain silly. If our friend Lorna had taken a sudden liking to Rolls-Royces, well . . .

In a little while we shall examine a collection of gimmicks from which you may be able to select one suitable for yourself, or which may suggest others more pleasing to you. First, however, we shall discuss a few attributes that are more basic, as enthusiasm is. Parenthetically, it should be pointed out that gimmicks do not have to be as insubstantial as the ones already referred to. Some of the gimmicks we shall discuss will have the power not only to make you colorful and to stand out, but also to add beneficially to your basic personality structure.

Somewhat related to enthusiasm, but not as exciting to others as enthusiasm, is curiosity. Remember, I said curiosity, not nosiness. Two brief anecdotes, both true, will serve to explain.

Edward D. was invited out to dinner by his boss. This was the first time. They had both been working late and the dinner was intended to be something in the nature of a show of considerateness to a devoted employee with whom the boss had had little, if any, social contact.

During the course of the meal, the boss told Edward that he was planning to go fishing up in Maine. A person with little curiosity might have said, "That's nice. I hope you enjoy it." Such a comment would have been sufficient, and the boss would have considered it kind and adequate, and that would have been the end of it. But Edward was gifted with curiosity.

"I've often thought of going fishing," he said. "But isn't it dull?"

"Dull? Hell, no," said the boss. "I can't imagine anything more enjoyable."

"Well," said Edward, "I'd like to try. How do you go about it? Is it expensive to buy tackle? And how do you know what to buy and where to go?"

Curiosity about things that affect or interest others is, if it is truly curiosity and not nosiness, flattering, whether it is meant to be flattering or not. It places the one who knows in an ego-feeding position *vis-à-vis* the one who is curious. "Well," said the boss, "I suppose it is a little complicated in the beginning, but you could start off in a small way."

"But I hear so much about blues and bass and flies and weather and all that," said Edward, "that I would think you'd have to know something at the very start. For instance, what kind of tackle should I ask for? Where would I go to fish? How do you get a boat? What do you do when you get a bite? You see what I mean?"

The boss chuckled. "I've been fishing for so many years," he said, "that I've forgotten that it doesn't come naturally." He then went into a detailed exposition of the art of fishing, prompted now and again by an additional question. Finally he became so involved in making Edward understand that he said, "Tell you what. You're coming along with me this weekend. The best way to learn, I always say, is to do. I like the way you approach the thing. You'll be a good fisherman before you know it."

Edward has curiosity. He is never going to want for company. Everybody likes to be with someone who wants to know . . . if, that is, they know the answers. If Edward, out of a clear sky, had started to ask his boss questions about Picasso, he might have embarrassed him so that he'd be lucky to hold on to his job, much less go fishing with him.

The other story is about Julia F., who met a woman she knew in a bus. Julia had heard that the woman was having trouble with her husband. Julia thought she was the curious type, but actually she was nosy. "How is your husband?" asked Julia.

The woman stiffened, but the question was a normal one, so she said, "Fine, thank you."

"My husband and I are planning a trip to Europe," said Julia. "Where are you going this year?"

"I don't know yet."

"Do you vacation together with your husband? Some people like separate vacations. I don't. Neither does my husband."

By this time the woman sensed that Julia was prying and she shelled up. You may be certain that thereafter she crossed to the other side of the street whenever she saw Julia coming her way.

Develop curiosity. Suppress nosiness.

Earlier in this volume we referred to desirable personality traits that everyone takes for granted, like honesty, generosity, cleanliness, considerateness and the like. Such traits are known to all and there is no intention here of belaboring them. What we are concerned with are attributes that are less frequently thought of and so too frequently forgotten. In this category, after enthusiasm and curiosity, we find also directness—not to be confused with tactlessness.

A direct person is always colorful and always stands out because most people are evasive and cautious. Directness is not a trait that can be easily acquired, nor is it suitable to every personality. Sometimes, indeed, it is a dangerous trait, because not all people can bear directness. Nevertheless, the rewards of directness can be so great that we should not pass it by without some consideration.

If you are the sort of person who can carry off directness, there is one rule that will save you from its dangers:

never, never, never be direct at the cost of kindness or considerateness. To pay with one fundamental personality trait for another is to pay too high a price.

In the old days Hollywood produced many movies about dowager aunts and chairbound uncles who were so colorful as a result of their directness that the public clamored for more and more of them. They weren't always so pleasing to their nieces and nephews, but the point is that directness was so colorful that it once was responsible for a movie vogue. Even today the crusty, direct relative is a box-office draw. If Lionel Barrymore were alive, he'd be one of the biggest things on television. You will recall that most of these crusty characters turned out to be, in the end, people of goodwill and kind heart—diamonds in the rough, so to speak—and that made them quite acceptable.

If you *are* a kind and considerate person, people will know it; and if people know you are basically kind and considerate, they will tend to accept bluntness from you; and if you are one who can be direct in an acceptable way, you will stand out in your circle.

The thing that people like about directness is that they know just where they stand with you. Directness gives them, more often than not, a sense of security, which is a treasure beyond price to a human being. For instance, if you are one who can say to a friend, "That hat is not for you and I'm sorry you bought it" and get away with it, that friend isn't going to have a doubt in the world when you say, "Now *that* is a hat that was made for you." On the other hand, if you always say, whether you like it or not, "That's a very nice hat," your words and comments become meaningless after a while, and the hatted one never knows whether the hat pleases you or not. They won't dislike you if you are always indirect in such things. They'll simply disregard you. You will be one of the nice colorless ones.

I was very hesitant about including this personality trait because of its dangers. For instance, a direct person at a staff meeting might lose his job because of his directness. Take this situation:

Boss: It is my feeling that we should change our inventory system to conform with that of Rowe & Company. They seem to be doing better with theirs than we are with ours.

Employee A: Seems like a good idea to me.

Employee B: Sounds good, but shouldn't we explore the matter a little? There may be some differences in our products that would make the Rowe system ineffective for us.

Employee C: I vote for a change.

Employee D: Some people have told me that Rowe isn't doing as well as appears on the surface. Maybe we'd better check on that.

Employee E, the direct one: I don't like the idea at all. Our method is the best one for us and I'm opposed completely to the change.

Employee E was right about the matter, but Mr. Boss was not the kind to stand for E's sort of directness. E didn't last very long after that. A poll of the others would have brought out the fact that they all agreed secretly with E. A and C were being sycophantic, while B and D were being cautious. It would have been to the benefit of the firm to accept E's judgment but it didn't work out that way.

On the other hand, if the boss had been a more secure person, he would have admired E's directness. E would have taken a special place in his mind and would have been in line for advancement because of his directness. The boss would have said to himself, "Now here's a man who says what he thinks. He doesn't try to butter me up and he doesn't play it safe. I will always know just where I stand with him. He can be a great asset to us."

Note that in either event, E stood out in the crowd. If you are one for taking a chance, take a chance on directness. You may lose some friends, but if you heed the cautionary note, you will make more friends than you lose. Every social group needs a curmudgeon for its own health, and a curmudgeon is merely a man who says what he thinks. Curmudgeons who can stand the risks and failure *always* come out on top in a crowd because they are the rarest of all *good* human beings. Just one thing: you won't be a very good curmudgeon if you are small and dainty. Curmudgeons have to be rather big to carry it off, or at the very least, venerable and wrinkled.

There is a fourth little-discussed personality trait that can be acquired by anybody without risk. I call it preferenceability, for there does not seem to be an official me for it. Preferenceability is the capacity for expressing preference without too much delay.

What is this power that preferenceability has to make stand out in our small crowd?

Many mothers know how annoying it is to ask a child hether he wants steak or chicken for dinner only to be ld, "It makes no difference to me—just make whatever easier." The mother wants to please her child (or her usband, as the case may be) and there is little satisfacon in serving a meal to which there is such an indifferent action. It isn't that the child or husband doesn't have a eference. Everybody always has a preference. What few eople have is preferenceability—the ability to express e preference at once. In the case we are discussing, if e mother says, "O.K., then, we'll have chicken," more ten than not the child or husband will say, "No, I guess d rather have steak after all." By this time all the fun has ne out of it for the mother.

Your position among people with whom you come in ntact will be greatly enhanced if you develop, as you sily can, the ability to express a preference as soon as u are questioned. It is so difficult for any group of peo- le to make up their minds about what movie to see, or hat gift to buy for an office colleague, or where to go on outing, or practically anything of minor importance, at if there is one person around who has a definite reference, he makes it easier for everyone. The beauty of is that it is not necessary to insist once you have expressed your preference. If it happens that there is a stronger preference among the others, you can yield gracefully with little loss. Most of the time, however, you will find that by deciding quickly you have solved the problem for all concerned, and if you become known as one who has definite preferences you will find that this attribute, too, has the quality of magnetism.

Preferenceability is even more important and more rewarding when it is merely a matter of answering a question like what you would prefer for dinner: "Which of these two hats do you like on me?"—"What would you like for your birthday, an umbrella or a purse?"—"Would you rather come to see me on Friday or on Sunday?"—et cetera. If you hesitate and say "Either one" or "It doesn't matter" or "Whatever suits you best" or something like that you create a problem for the other person, and though the problem may be a small one it registers on the mind and after many such answers to a given person you become associated in his mind in a vague way with problems and annoyance.

If, on the other hand, you say at once, "I like that one," or "You're very kind—I'd prefer an umbrella," or "Let's make it Sunday," you are solving a problem for the other person, and people just gravitate to those who make things easier for them.

It's the promptness of the expression of preference that counts, for if you answer at once it appears that you are so sure of your preference that you don't even have to think about it. That makes the other person sure he i pleasing you, and he always feels good about the ability to do that.

Try it and see how easy it is. Oddly enough, you will find that most of the time you will be expressing your true preference, for that is the way the mind works when it works without pondering. If, on occasion, you say you prefer something you really do not prefer, what have you lost? These things are all so unimportant in your life that the gain to your personality image easily outweighs them.

Now, visualize yourself as a man or a woman who is enthusiastic, who is curious, who is direct and who has decided preferences. Could the average person who is none of these things (and the average person *is* none of these things) fail to notice you, or consider you an unusual person, or be drawn to you? The answer is no. Even if you leave out directness, the answer will still be no.

We have reached the point at which we should enlarge on the matter of gimmicks, those little tricks that serve as trademarks and which add the bizarre bit of color to your personality that so happily complements the more fundamental qualities that make you stand out.

The possibilities are endless and our space is limited, so here again we can only point the way with a few examples, any one of which can set your mind to working on a hundred variations. Gimmicks are of two sorts: physical and non-physical. La Guardia's big hat, Roosevelt's cigarette holder, Churchill's cigar and the like are physical. Lorna's enthusiasm for ivory elephants is a combination of physical and non-physical, for her pleasure in the elephants is as important as the elephants themselves. Truman's walks are in the non-physical category, for there is no physical object involved though the walks themselves are physical actions. Jack Benny's stinginess is clearly non-physical.

It would be easy to invent a number of gimmicks, but I have seen enough of them in use to tell you about real ones that have actually been employed. The first that comes to mind is a non-physical one developed by an office secretary. One day, at lunch, she said to the two girls who were with her: "It's crazy to eat at this hour. The place is crowded, the service is bad, and it's too noisy. Tomorrow I'll eat later."

She had intended to have her lunch the next day at two-thirty, after the big rush, but she got tied up with some urgent letters and did not get out until three. "You're crazy," said the other girls and she thought that maybe they were right. But the restaurant was so peaceful, and the service was so good, that she made up her mind then and there to lunch at three P.M. in the future. The next morning she delayed breakfast until her ten-thirty coffee break and went to lunch at three. That meant also delaying dinner from the usual seven until eight o'clock.

She continued the routine for a week and was about to go back to the old schedule when she was introduced by one of the girls to a visitor as the "three-o'clock-lunch girl." This so intrigued the visitor that he gave her considerably more attention than he might otherwise have done. Something clicked in her mind and she did not change back. Now the three o'clock lunch is her permanent trademark and it is a gimmick that has served her well. There is no immutable law of nature that dictates the hours of meals.

I know a young man who collects the front pages of newspapers. He cannot afford to buy all the papers published in his area, so his friends save the front pages of their own papers for him. They all get more pleasure out of their papers, for that which they used to throw away has now become a gift which they can use to give pleasure to front-page Charlie. When they travel, they make a special project of bringing home for Charlie the front pages of out-of-town or foreign newspapers, and this adds to the enjoyment of their travels.

Not long ago I was introduced to a man who has had two hats for more than twenty years, has worn them throughout that period, and refuses ever to buy a new hat. This gimmick borders on the freakish, but it doesn't quite cross the line. He keeps the hats cleaned and blocked, and though they show signs of wear, they are not sloppy. These hats have been very good to him, having taken him out of the mass of two billion, nine hundred and ninety-nine million, into the club of nine hundred and eighty or ninety thousand colorful little people.

There is a woman in New York State who takes a four-second colored movie shot of a tulip tree in her back yard every sunny morning. She has been doing it for a number of years and if you can get into her good graces she will show you one of the most fascinating movies you ever saw—a movie of a tree actively growing before your eyes from a tiny stem to a sturdy fifteen-foot-high tree. Tulip trees grow very tall and her gimmick will serve her for her lifetime. Everybody in the neighborhood gets a tingle of pleasure out of telling about her to strangers. She is considered to be a very colorful member of the community.

Neville Chamberlain, once Prime Minister of England, used to carry an umbrella with him every time he went out. That is not too unusual in England, but an executive of my acquaintance in the United States has borrowed the gimmick. At first he did it because he was a very cautious man. Now he does it for two reasons—because he is a cautious man and also because he finds it to be a wonderful icebreaker. People never fail to comment humorously on his umbrella and the mood is good the moment he comes onto the scene.

A high school girl in my community has a brother who was given a ten-dollar tie. He didn't like it and he told her she could give it to one of her boy friends. "Give away a ten-dollar tie!" she exclaimed. "I'd have to love a boy to do that."

"Well," said her brother, "why don't you just lend it to someone?"

Laughingly she told the girls about it at school. The girls passed the story along. The next morning one of the boys approached her and said, "I hear you have a ten dollar tie you're willing to lend. Lend it to me and I'll take you to a movie Saturday night." It was a huge joke to him, but she reacted promptly. "O.K.," she said, and he took her to the movies, wearing the borrowed tie. The story got around still more and within two weeks the gag swept the school. Dozens of boys were asking for dates with the proviso that they could wear the ten-dollar tie. The gimmick won't last forever, but it certainly illustrates the value of gimmicks.

Surely you get the idea. Surely you can find a trademark that suits you and fits you. Many of the gimmicks in use developed through accident, but they don't have to be accidental and they don't have to be freakish like that of Walter B., who tries to achieve color by wearing shoes that don't match.

Remember, a gimmick will always attract attention and make you stand out when it first becomes known, but it can be of permanent service only if it be in addition to and not instead of the fundamental qualities we all look for in a person we would like to have as a friend. Churchill would be just another fat man with a cigar if it were not for his brilliance, his courage, his eloquence and his innate decency. And you could be just another nobody with a transiently interesting gimmick if you lack the basic attributes of a desirable human being.

So use a gimmick as an aid, if you want to and if you can, but never lean on it all the way or you will surely come a cropper.

Chapter Six

SKELETONS IN YOUR CLOSET

❦ Can you keep a secret? If you can, you have a very desirable personality trait that will help you to make friends; that is, if you don't overdo it. Sometimes you can go to jail for keeping a secret, as when you keep from the police your knowledge of a crime. Sometimes you can lose all your friends by being too secretive: when you make a secret of almost everything, people begin to feel you don't trust them. And sometimes a penchant for secrecy leads others to the belief that you are hiding guilt, and so *they* won't trust *you*.

There is another kind of secrecy that is rarely discussed and that is quite divorced from anything mentioned above. It is the secrecy engendered by fear—fear that feeds on itself and becomes eternal. More often than not the original fear is unfounded, yet untold thousands of men and women live out their lives unfulfilled, unhappy and incomplete because of their unwillingness to bring the fear out into the open, face it and do something about it. It becomes a skeleton in the closet of life, and the owner of the skeleton lives in constant fear that someone may some day open the closet and see it.

Sixteen hundred years ago a wise Oriental Christian named Syrus said: "You are in a pitiable condition when you have to conceal what you wish to tell." Most of the time those with skeletons in their closets desire with all their being to tell about them, but refrain because of silly, unreasoning fear that their friends and neighbors will not understand, or will condemn or turn against them.

Give the rest of the world a chance to prove its decency. Don't assume that everyone you know is waiting in ambush to pounce upon you as soon as it becomes known that your engagement ring is worth only fifty dollars, or that you rented your tuxedo, or that you have a red birthmark on your back, or that your hair would be black if you hadn't changed the color, or that one of your relatives spent time in jail.

What is your answer now if I ask whether you can keep a secret? It depends, doesn't it, on what kind of a secret it is? If it is the skeleton type, open the closet door wide. It's far better that way. Your personality is at its best when you are free of self-created anxieties and embarrassments. You can't project a likable image when a part of your mind is always in the shadow of fear of "discovery." You will be pleased to see how much more engaging people will consider you if you are not always on guard before the locked door of your skeleton closet.

Here's a little secret: most of these closets have glass doors. It is only your imagination that makes you believe you are the only one who can see through the door of your own closet. If you pretend there are no skeletons in there, everybody will go along with your little game and pretend with you. But they'll be so much more comfortable with you when you make it unnecessary for them to pretend. And even if some of your skeletons are actually invisible to the rest of the world, the price of keeping them unseen is too high.

Perhaps there are no skeletons in your closet, nagging at you night and day. If that is the case, move on to the next chapter. On the other hand, perhaps you don't recognize a skeleton when you see one. Following are twenty-five questions about commonly locked-up skeletons. Are any of them in *your* closet?

1. *Do you smile only half-smiles or hold your hand before your mouth when you speak because you have a crooked or a missing tooth or because you are afraid your breath is—well—you know?*
A dentist or a doctor would set your personality free.

2. *Are you ashamed of your parents and do you keep them away from your friends?*
What seems simply terrible to you may seem charming to others. At worst they would sympathize rather than

think less of you if you took your parents out of the closet.

3. *Do you try to convince your friends you are more important in your job than you really are, and does that make it impossible for you to let them visit you at the office or meet your boss or co-workers? Do you try to keep up with the Joneses?*

People usually know when you are bluffing about your station in life. They have contempt, rather than admiration, for those who put on an act. It is an act of self-confidence to be yourself, and if you project yourself as you really are you'll be much more at ease and you'll have much more fun. Who knows, such self-confidence may even help your career advancement and make you more important in your job. After a while the Joneses may have to keep up with *you*.

4. *Do you overtax your strength because you are ashamed to show weakness?*

Some folks are stronger than others. That is one of the facts of life. You'll never enjoy yourself while worrying about the fact that your fun is killing you. In this age of dieting and health-consciousness you'll be right in the swim if you take care of yourself. It is quite possible, too, that your friends will welcome a change of pace themselves.

5. *When you are with people whose speech is better than yours do you affect an unnatural accent?*

If you do, you will have to give so much thought to your manner of speech that you will neglect the content and quite likely make a fool of yourself. One of our greatest playwrights speaks what is known as "Brooklynese." He has said that for a time he tried to affect a more cultured accent but gave it up when he discovered people wanted him for what he was rather than for how he pronounced his words. This is not to say that you should not make an effort to improve your speech if it be sloppy but rather that you do it gradually, as it comes naturally to you.

6. *Do you hide the fact that you have been divorced?*

If the fact is an impediment, face it and get it over with. You can't please everybody and if you keep the skeleton in the closet you'll be so conscious of it that you may please nobody.

7. *Do you wear padded bras?*

They won't help at the moment of truth, and you'll spend your life worrying about that moment of truth and because of that perhaps never get to it. You'll feel so much freer when you know the boys are seeing you as you really are that your personality may be radiant enough to compensate for what you imagine you are lacking. Most of the world's greatest actresses project more personality than bosom, and they get by very well. Why not you?

8. *Do you drink though you hate it and it makes you sick?*

Just speak up at the next party and say: "I hate this stuff and it makes me sick." You'll get the surprise of your life. Try it.

9. *Do you wear a toupee?*
Whom do you think you are kidding? Not a soul, actually. Your bald head, naked, is more attractive than your bald head clothed with someone else's hair; and two minutes after you've been introduced you can get your head off your mind. You can never forget your pate as long as there's a wig on it. That is, if you are a man. Women are different.

10. *Are you afraid to step on a scale in the presence of your friends?*
Remember, they can *see* you, off the scale as well as on. Either recognize your stoutness and put your friends at ease, or let a doctor help you take off some weight. This is one skeleton you can't hide in a closet.

11. *Are you always worried that a new boy friend will find out about an indiscretion with an old one?*
Confess and stop worrying. If you lose him—well, better now than later and better because *you* told him than another. And don't commit any more indiscretions. Word of virtue gets around just as fast as word of error. And you feel so *free!*

12. *Are you suppressed and nervous and depressed*

because you are avid and don't want your husband to know it lest he consider you wanton?

How little you know your husband. Remember: be yourself and you'll be free enough to be magnetic.

13. *Has there been mental illness in your family and does that inhibit your social relationships?*

In this enlightened day only unintelligent people look on mental illness as something to be hidden. Intelligent people know that it is an illness that requires treatment and that if it is to be conquered it must be kept out in the open rather than hidden in a closet with skeletons. There is so large an incidence of mental illness that if every family harboring a victim were to withdraw from social contact, the entire complexion of social intercourse would be altered.

14. *Are you keeping secret the knowledge of your wife's or husband's transgression because you don't want to break up the family?*

The most unfortunate family is one that is held together under the shadow of suspicion or hatred or blame or anger or all combined. Bring the skeleton out into the open. Forgive the transgression if you can. And then start over in a more normal atmosphere. If you can't forgive, it is fairer to all concerned that a parting take place.

15. *Have you ever been convicted of a crime and are you now fearful that if your friends find out they will discard you?*

Those who have paid the penalty for their crimes have redeemed their debt to society. That's the law of the land as well as the gospel of religion. This skeleton is, nevertheless, one of the most difficult to expose because many people will condemn even those who have paid their debt. Employers, too, are often unfair about it. If the disease is better than the cure, it is unwise to be cured. You'll have to assess your own position and make a judgment. If you can function fairly well with the skeleton locked in the closet, perhaps you should go along as you are now going along. One thing should be considered: friends who are truly friends remain friends, and friendship blossoms best in a climate of total faith and honesty.

16. Are you illegitimate?

Keep the skeleton in the closet and forget about it. Society has not yet advanced to the point of not blaming little babies for being born out of wedlock. Only before marriage should you expose this skeleton; and then you must do it even if it means the marriage is off. You could not possibly live a normal and happy married life with that skeleton always threatening you, though you can be normal and happy in all your other social relationships. If your love is mutual and real, the knowledge will not stand in the way of either marriage or happiness.

17. Have you changed your name?

Don't announce the fact every time you are introduced to someone, but mention it frankly if the occasion is appropriate. Authors use pen names, actors use stage names, and the whole world knows it and doesn't care. What makes you think they will make a federal case out of your adopted name? Throw this skeleton out at once and be free.

18. *Are you hiding your true religion or race?*
The price for this is much too high for the "value" received. Not only do you miss the deep joy of identification with your own religion, your own culture and your own people, you miss as well any chance of real identification with others. Set the record straight and learn what real living is.

19. *Do you have an adopted child and do you live in fear that the child will discover the truth?*
Most people have learned that this skeleton doesn't belong in a closet. They tell their adopted children the facts and explain that while other parents take what they get, the parents of adopted children have taken them in by choice. Having disposed of the skeleton, they are then able to communicate freely and without the shadow of dread. It is not fair to saddle any child with a parent who constantly fears the truth.

20. *Are you one of those wives who keep a private, secret fund of money from her husband's knowledge?*
You'll never enjoy it as long as you are worried about the fact that he may find out about it, and you will al-

ways be worried about that. If it is a moderate amount, spend it on a present for him tomorrow. If it is a substantial sum, confess and place it in your joint account. He'll love you even more than he did before and you will be free at last.

21. *Do you refuse to wear glasses or a hearing aid though you have difficulty with your sight or hearing?*

You may think you have this skeleton locked in the closet but the door is always wide open. The real reason for vanity is the desire for admiration, but all you win for your vanity in this case is ridicule. Help your sight or hearing with the proper aids and come back into the world. It's far more beautiful than you ever imagined without them. If Bernard Baruch wears a hearing aid and that lovely sex-actress wears glasses, who do you think *you* are? As for men not making passes at girls who wear glasses, that was a generation ago.

22. *Are you inhibited in your relationships because you feel sex is unclean or indecent?*

It isn't. Seek professional advice and treatment. Until you do, your personality will be inadequate in all other types of relationship as well.

23. *Are you an alcoholic or a dope addict?*

Even if you manage to function well enough most of the time to hide it from your friends and associates, you are never more than half alive and you are missing most

of the true joys and satisfactions that life offers. And
sooner or later your skeleton will be exposed and you will
be completely shattered. The solution is obvious. Go to
your doctor for help.

24. *Are you living in adultery?*

Instead of having twice as much fun you are not having half as much, for you are living in constant fear that
your closet door will be opened. Your fear will color all
of your emotions and activities and your personality will
become a distorted imitation of the real thing. In this case,
do not expose the skeleton—eliminate it entirely by eliminating the cause of its existence.

25. *Do you wear shoes that are too small for you?*

If you do, did you ever stop to think that you couldn't
get your feet into shoes that were more than a trifle
smaller? It is foolish to imagine that people will see you
differently if your shoes are one size larger. Why pay with
pain and discomfort that imprison your personality for
what is at best an imaginary advantage?

There we have twenty-five big and little skeletons of
assorted shapes and sizes out of thousands that are hidden in closets all over the land. Now that you know what
a skeleton is, perhaps you will discover some of your own
that you never consciously imagined to be skeletons.

I have used the word "free" over and over and over
again in this chapter because in terms of personality de-

SKELETONS IN YOUR CLOSET 121

velopment the freer you are from fears and secrets that inhabit your attitudes and activities the less likely you are to fall short of adequacy in your social contacts. So get the skeletons out of your closet and send them into limbo. Be free.

Chapter Seven

DON'T LIVE ALONE IF YOU DON'T LIKE IT

> All alone
> By the telephone,
> Waiting for a ring,
> A ting-a-ling . . .

❦ Do you remember that song? It was one of the big hits in the year in which it was published. The reason for its extraordinary success was the fact that it hit the nail right on the head for so many, many lonely people. I recall, with some self-reproach, an unkind vision I had at the time—a vision of ten million lost souls sitting alone in ten million barren rooms by ten million telephones, each of the ten million lost souls waiting for a ring, a ting-a-ling. If each one, I thought, were to call a telephone number entirely at random, the laws of chance alone would connect at least five hundred thousand of them, one with another, and take at least that number out of their misery.

It seemed to be a fact then, and it seems equally true now, that most people do not like living alone. One wonders, however, why they go on living alone in the face of their unhappiness. One is reminded of another hit song in which one poor lonely soul took to living with a sort of spook: "Me and my shadow—all alone and feeling blue. Me and my shadow . . . not a soul to tell our troubles to."

There are, of course, many hardy souls who like to live alone so much that they wouldn't change even for love and marriage. These are the truly self-sufficient ones who have the courage to face four walls in solitude night after night after night, fortified with the philosophical attitudes that mark the professional hermits of the world. Such hardy individuals are deserving only of the highest degree of admiration tinged with awe. Most people of lesser breed—like you and me, for example—were born to blossom best in cohabitation with other human beings. If we don't live with people, we tend to lose some of our livelier traits and to take on some of the characteristics of the inanimate objects with which we do live—like telephones and walls and shadows, perhaps. If it is an outgoing, magnetic personality we seek to develop, we shall not develop it in conditions of complete aloneness every night. It is more constructive for your personality for you to come home to someone every night, even if it be a landlady and a boarder to whom you never say a word, than it is to open your door on complete nothingness.

At this point it would be easy to advise those who are living alone to start living with one or more others and then go on to the next chapter. If you are one of those who are now living alone, however, you know that it is not quite so simple a matter. Everything in life exacts its price and this aspect of life is no exception. There are many advantages to living alone and whole books have been written about these advantages. (One wonders, sometimes, whether the necessity for such books is not in itself a revelation of the fact that live-aloners are so conscious of a lack that they must be periodically reassured that they are happy.) What you must do is to weigh the advantages against the emptiness and decide for yourself which is heavier.

"I like living alone," said an acquaintance of mine. "I really do. I like the privacy; I like the freedom to come and go as I please without the feeling that I am disturbing others; I like the ability to invite whom I wish to invite whenever I wish it; I like the liberty to let the cleaning go when I'm not in the mood for housework; I like freedom to lounge about in whatever state of dress or undress I choose; I like the right to play the piano or my hi-fi as loudly as I see fit; I like the feeling that everything in my home is mine and mine alone."

Now it cannot be denied that all these things are in a sense desirable. But so is lots of money and so is fame and so is expensive perfume and so is travel. The hitch is the unalterable fact that nothing that you can get out of your life is completely satisfying if it is for yourself alone. We are so constituted that we *must* share to enjoy, unless we are born to be hermits and develop the philosophy of hermits. It is true, as we saw earlier, that there are times when solitude is a refreshing gift, but solitude is like pepper and salt—good as a seasoning for life and bad when taken in large and constant doses.

In answer to that my acquaintance says: "You are overdramatizing my situation. I am not a hermit. I share my home and my possessions and even my bed whenever I feel the need. At other times I have my privacy and my complete freedom of action. I have the best of both possible worlds."

"O.K.," I reply. "Go right ahead. I still think you are kidding yourself."

Sharing cannot be turned on and off like the water in your tap. Even the sharing about which my acquaintance speaks is a selfish act, turned on and off for selfish reasons. It cannot give the joy and satisfaction of sharing for the sake of sharing, because one has an urge to give as well as to receive. The capacity for such sharing comes only from living with others. Ask an only child how he views a family of seven brothers and sisters; even a child understands.

The best kind of living together is family living together. Men and women should marry, have children and experience all of the joys and the worries and the excitements and the confusions and the frustrations and the ecstasies and the quarrels and the despairs and the hopes of family life. This is man at his most complete, his most fulfilled. The lone genius does more for the world but far less for himself and for his own happiness. The family man (or woman, of course) may not have the capacity for improving the world but he accomplishes that which is beyond the competence of the greatest of lonely geniuses: he builds a little island in the vast sea of humanity on which dwell a few people who, together, live lives of such depth and social creativity that live-aloners may not even be able to understand them, though more often than not they are either consciously or unconsciously envious. No family person ever—except, perhaps, in rare moments of great trouble or tragedy—envies a live-aloner. (We must not take into account the periods of exceptional stress or worry, for they cancel each other out in the lives of both sorts of people. If a family man, in a time of trouble, wishes for a while that he were alone in the world, it is also true that the live-aloner who is ill or in trouble misses more than anything else the presence in his life of dear ones who consider his troubles their own. This is far from being the same as the sympathy, consideration and assistance of outsiders.)

Though I believe that family life is the best kind of life, I know that not all people can have the best of anything that life offers. There are many, many people who for one or another good and sufficient reason do not look forward to the possibility of lives of family togetherness. You may be one of them; but the fact that you cannot have the best is no reason for depriving yourself of the nearest to the best that you can get. A large family is better than a small one; one child is better than no child; a husband or a wife alone is better than no husband or wife; a friend is better than a stranger; a stranger is better than no one; a dog or a cat or a bird is better than nothing whatever. (Telephones and walls and shadows don't rate at all.) A human being should always be able to come home to someone or something living and loving—at the very least, living. The knowledge that he is in a position to do so colors his every thought and word and act. It makes him a different, a warmer, a more attractive personality. Greatness and respect and admiration can come to the live-aloner; affection comes to those who know how to live with others.

In moments of sharpest self-communion, affection is warmer than admiration, more deeply satisfying than respect and more rewarding than the knowledge of greatness.

"All right," you may say, "let us concede that it is better not to live alone. What should I do about it? Should I put an ad in the paper offering to share my apartment? Should I move to a boardinghouse? Tell me."

The answer is that it does not matter much what course of action you take so long as you do it intelligently. There are people who, when they tired of living alone, took steps to share their lives and then decided that they liked it better the old way. The fact that as a general rule it is better to live with someone else than to live alone does not make it equally a fact that in every specific case the general rule will apply. Obviously it is better to live alone, for example, than to live with a dirty, or a hateful, or a cruel, or a boorish person. What you should do is accept the principle of the superiority of shared living and then work out the details in the most desirable and rewarding manner.

The most commonly followed procedure is that of apartment sharing. A girl who has an apartment will find another girl to share it with her. A man who wants to share an apartment will rent one in collaboration with another. What follows? The wonderful life of togetherness about which I have been writing in such glowing terms? It would be gratifying to be able to answer affirmatively and go on to the next subject. Unfortunately, as you must know if you have had the opportunity to speak with a number of people who share apartments, it doesn't always work out precisely according to the blueprint. You hear more complaints about fellow tenants than praise.

The reason for this is not hard to find: careless abuse of a good idea.

Apartment sharers should be selected as carefully as husbands or wives. The extremely jealous man who marries a gorgeous flirt is putting misery rather than happiness into the bank of life. The delicate, sensitive, cultured girl who chooses a husband who is illiterate, insensitive and sloppy would do better to live in the forest as a hermit. These things are true despite the fact that *in general* family living is the happiest living. So is it true that it is far better to live alone and try to like it than to share an apartment with a cell mate who cannot possibly be a soul mate.

Sharing an apartment should be worked out as one would negotiate a business deal, for after all, the business of living is the most important business of all. The difference is that the rewards of successful shared living are calculated in terms of ease, comfort and happiness rather than in terms of money.

A few pages back we considered the comments of my acquaintance who outlined a number of the advantages to be gained by living alone: privacy, the freedom to come and go at will, the right to invite friends according to whim or fancy, to play music at a high-decibel rate and let the housework go, the feeling of total possession, etc. We agreed that these were genuine advantages.

In sharing an apartment one might have to surrender some of these advantages. For instance, one could no longer have total privacy or total possession. On the other hand, there is no need to surrender all of them. Good business would dictate the assurance of the largest possible profit which, in this case, would be the retention of as many of the advantages as can possibly be retained while at the same time acquiring the new advantages afforded by the fact of having someone to come home to. Contrary to the situation in ordinary business deals, however, it does not follow that your profit is someone else's loss.

All of this can be boiled down to a simple sentence:

when you share an apartment, share it with someone whose interests, habits and attitudes are as much like your own as possible.

If you are living alone, presumably your situation is not so desperate that you must change it by nine o'clock tomorrow morning. Give yourself time—lots of time, if necessary. Talk the matter out at length with your prospective co-tenant. State your own position frankly. Tell about those of your customs that might possibly annoy or disturb certain types of people. Mention your likes and dislikes. Tell as much about yourself as you would like to know about the other, and then ask for an equally frank response. Remember, you will both have to be living together in very intimate relationship and you won't have the bond of love that may make even unsuitable marriages work on occasion.

When you find the right person you will know it almost at once. Rapport will come quickly and be followed by enthusiasm. Did you ever watch a hi-fi enthusiast meeting another one? Or observe two dieters in conversation? Or hear the unending talk of two golf bugs? When people of like interests come together, the problem of congeniality does not exist. Thus if my much-talked-about acquaintance were to have as a co-tenant one who likes loud music, who doesn't care that the place may be messy on occasion, who sleeps through late homecomings and door openings and shuttings, who also likes privacy and is willing to give it as well as receive it periodically, who thinks a lounging robe is as attractive as formal dress—why, in that case my acquaintance would be retaining almost all of her present advantages and at the same time would be receiving the great boon of having someone congenial to come home to most of the time.

On the other hand, if my acquaintance were to advertise for a sharer and take the first one who offered to pay half the bills, the result might be a large net loss in terms of comfort and happiness. The sharer might be allergic to noise, pathologically neat, and unbearably prudish. Then my acquaintance would be really in a mess.

Next to family living, sharing an apartment on equal terms with a congenial person is the best way to conquer the loneliness that is the direct result of living alone rather than the result of some other influence such as shyness, the loss of loved ones, social inadequacy, etc. There are other ways to conquer this loneliness, however, and we shall now examine them, keeping always in mind several basic truths that bear repetition:

1. In general, it is better to live with people than to live alone.

2. In specific, it is better to live alone than to live with people who make you unhappy by reason of uncongeniality, cruelty, intolerance, etc.

3. Loneliness is a complex experience. It can overwhelm you in the midst of tens or hundreds of other people, and it can be absent at times when you are completely alone. You must have in yourself sufficient resources to be alone for reasonable periods of time; and you must have in yourself the capacity for enjoying the

company of others and giving them enjoyment in your companionship for extended periods of time.

The second most frequently employed method of avoiding cohabitation with a shadow and a telephone is that of moving to a hotel. In a hotel the clerk greets you when you return, there is a telephone operator who knows you, a floor maid takes care of your room or your suite and keeps it shipshape, and there are bellhops who hop when you ring the bell. Quite a lot of nice people to come home to, *n'est-ce pas?* I, for one, would rather live alone in an apartment.

Hotel living can be wonderful for couples. It can be bearable for families. It can be luxurious and pleasant for a night or two or even for a week or two when you are all alone. Throughout the length and breadth of the land you will find more lonely people in hotels than anywhere else. My heart always goes out in pity for traveling sales men (in the stories they live gay and glamorous lives of constant companionship) sitting in hotel lobbies night after night, either in solitary longing for home or in forced conversation with other, equally lonely, drummer of trade. I have done it myself many times, and those have been my loneliest times.

Do you know, as I know, any elderly men or women who live alone in hotel rooms, trying to get into conversation with others in the same boat so they can tell about letter they got from the children? Students of geriatric have long known how devastating this form of living can be and they have evolved systems of community living for senior citizens that save them from such utter loneliness.

The word that best applies to hotel life is transience, which is defined in the best unabridged dictionary as: "quality or state of being transient, fleeting or shifting; transitoriness; as, the *transience* of human life or time." Though you may be a permanent resident of a hotel, most of the guests are transient—they come and go, fleeting and shifting like human life and time—adding to loneliness rather than decreasing it. (I am not referring, of course, to completely residential hotels, which are merely modified forms of apartment dwellings.) The only way I can account for the widespread custom of living alone in hotels is to assume that those who live thus are either completely self-sufficient or are brainwashed by certain forms of propaganda. And lest anyone imagine that these comments may be damaging to the hotel business, I suggest that you try to get a reservation in a good hotel at the last moment. (Why worry about bad hotels?)

A far better choice, though not as good as apartment sharing, is a room with a private family or in a boardinghouse. This would be a better choice if only for the reason that it eliminates the word "transience" from the constant scene.

Most private families who let out a room or two are composed of very nice and friendly people who need the rent money and who will always do their level best to keep their tenants comfortable and happy. You can get to know them well and even to become, in a sense, a part of the family. Much will depend on your willingness to accept their friendship. I know some people who have rented rooms with private families and who always feel as though they are intruders. They come in quietly in the evening and rush into the solitude of the rooms they have rented. For them there is little companionship and they come home to shadow and telephone like the live-aloners. I know others who meet the families halfway and who are very happy in their tenancy. In some cases genuine affection has developed and there are exchanges of birthday, anniversary and Christmas gifts. In these cases living in a rented room has become almost like living with family. The trick is to pick the family intelligently as well as the room, and then, as I have said, to meet the family halfway.

Boardinghouses, too, offer great opportunities for companionship. Boarders are comparatively permanent dwellers and they can, and often do, become very good friends. Among boarders there are the bickerings and the complaints and the problems that arise in ordinary family living, but there are also the caring about one another and the intimacies and affection that are inherent in family life. The best procedure in establishing yourself as a tenant of a boardinghouse is that of trial and error. Take a place for two weeks. If it turns out well, stay. If you don't care for it, move and try to find what you seek in another one. Sooner or later you will strike it rich. Incidentally, more girl and boy friends and more wedding and more career and business opportunities come out of boardinghouses than you would think. Even if the tenants themselves don't qualify, many of them have friends and relatives who do.

Beyond these traditional forms of living with people there are others which are limited only by the drive and ingenuity of those who seek them. In Cambridge, Massachusetts, which is, as you know, a college town, there lived a retired middle-aged schoolteacher in a six-room apartment. Loneliness was her only companion and it was, you may be certain, an unwelcome one. All her life she had been accustomed to the presence and the love and resentment and annoyance and gratitude of her students. Without them, and in the absence of kin, she hardly cared to go on.

"I hate rattling around in this big apartment all alone," she once told a friend in another city who had telephoned to wish her a Happy New Year.

"I'd hate it myself," said the caller. "Why don't you take in a few handsome boarders?"

The suggestion was made in jest, but it sparked an idea. The ex-teacher's apartment was near a college that was short of dormitory accommodations. Why could she not provide living quarters for a few students who were too late for the dorms? She fixed up three of her rooms so they would be suitable for two students each and in short order had them taken by three sets of roommates.

Now, as a sort of den mother, she no longer rattles around alone in her apartment. Sometimes the confusion and bedlam (she has only two bathrooms) are so great that she wonders whatever got into her to give up her peace and quiet for all this excitement; but in her calmer moments she remembers what the loneliness and emptiness were like before and she thanks her stars for the telephone call that started her on a new life. "Some day," she says, "I'll close off one of the rooms. It'll be quieter with only four boys." But semester follows semester and she never does.

The case of the ex-teacher is not one in which she found someone to come home to but, rather, one in which she found someone (and more than some*one*) to come home to her. Both needs are equally vital, but finding someone to come home to you has the added advantage often of financial gain. Our den mother no longer has to worry about her old-age needs. Most of the rent money goes right into the bank.

In preparing this chapter I have been inquiring of friends, relatives and strangers about their knowledge of other instances in which people who were living alone expanded their horizons and brought others into their lives. I have been amazed at the variety of the methods that have been employed. Space limitations forbid describing them at length, so we shall have to content ourselves with brief expositions of a few. These may serve to stimulate your thinking so that you may come up with a plan that will be best suited to your own situation, your own needs and your own talents.

1. A newspaper photographer who for many years lived an exciting life among all sorts of people at home

and abroad came finally to the day when he was retired. Unable to travel and mix with people any longer, he found himself unbearably lonely. As much as the people, he missed the stimulation that his camera had given him, for he loved photography. He solved his problem by investing his savings in an established photography school, entering the firm as a partner-teacher. He had no responsibility for the business phase of the school, so his activities remained well within his physical capacities. He still lives alone, but his days are filled with people and he gets tremendous satisfaction out of employing his expert professional knowledge creatively. If he desired shared living in the evening, he could easily resort to one of the traditional procedures.

2. A young widow, suddenly on her own, took a job in the hope that busyness would alleviate her loneliness. The days were tolerable for her but the nights were bleak. She did not want to share her apartment and she had no desire to live in a hotel or a boardinghouse. One evening she offered to baby-sit for some friends. They were very grateful and promised to be home before midnight so she could get a reasonable amount of time for sleeping. They got home on time but she sensed that they had had to leave just when the party they had been attending was becoming most enjoyable. It occurred to her that there must be many people who felt they were missing all the fun because they had to be bound by the time limitations imposed by baby-sitters. She advertised in a newspaper offering her services as a sleep-over baby-sitter and from

the responses selected three couples with charming children. She sits for them as required and averages three nights a week as a sleep-over sitter. She loves all of her children and derives a great deal of joy from her service. At the same time she always has a number of nights each week in the privacy of her own apartment—nights that are now enjoyable because they are a part of a changing scene rather than an endless way of life.

3. Four stenographers, all between twenty-two and twenty-five, who lived alone and didn't like it but at the same time could not bear to give up the privacy of their small apartments, were discussing the matter at lunch one day when one of them got what she called a brainstorm. "Why can't we all get apartments in the same building?" she asked. "Then, if any of us got the creeps at night, we'd have someone right there to go to . . . if convenient, of course." The others were enthusiastic. They had a most difficult time finding a building with four available apartments. The best they could discover was one with two apartments. They decided that two of the girls would move in and wait for vacancies for the others. It was a year and a half before they were all together under the same master TV aerial, but they did finally make it. Now they are a family of four, each living alone and all living together. They hardly ever get the "creeps" because the very knowledge that if they did cure would be right at hand usually serves as effective medicine.

4. A day worker who lived alone didn't like it. She

could have obtained a sleep-in job with a nice family, but she felt that to live with a family in the capacity of servant was not quite what one could call being a part of the family. If she could find a way to move in with a family as an equal and still draw the salary she needed, her difficulty would be overcome; but how did one manage to do anything as clever as that? She managed to do it. Indeed, she managed to move in as more than an equal and still draw her weekly check—a bigger check than ever. What she did was to learn practical nursing for mothers just out of hospital with newborn babies. She is constantly in demand, for the population, as you know, is exploding. Her average stay with a family is two months, with never a dull moment and with every moment filled with love for her very young charges, and often for their parents. She is looked up to and considered almost the head of the family in every case, and when she leaves, there are tears on both sides—the tears of family partings. For her, however, there is always a new family around the corner; and while it isn't like having her own family, it is far, far better than living alone.

Have you found the answer to your own loneliness problem here? If you have, go and do likewise. If not, do otherwise. But, I advise, do *something*. The world will see a brighter sparkle in your eyes if you live with people, ignore shadows and walls, and use the telephone for communication instead of companionship.

Chapter Eight

BOY MEETS GIRL

❦   We come now to a most sensitive area in your relationships with people—the area known as your love life. It is an important area as well as a sensitive one and it deserves a couple of chapters. However, you need have no fear, for we shall not invade the domain of the newspaper columnists who sacrificially devote their lives to giving advice to the lovelorn. We are working on personality development and the elimination of loneliness and we shall stick to our job.

We seek association with other people for a variety of reasons: we want friends, we want neighbors, we want colleagues, we want roommates, we want classmates, we want acquaintances and we want relatives. If we are normal we also want association with certain members of the opposite sex for no other reason than that they *are* of the opposite sex. First we like to "play the field" and then, after a while, we narrow the field down to a single person and, if we are fortunate, we marry that one and live happily ever after.

It sounds so simple. What a pity it is often so difficult.

To establish relationships with members of the opposite sex it is usually necessary to go through a process known as dating. Unfortunately this process, which should be a joy and a delight, is all too often the cause of frustration, perplexity and misery. Every night there are thousands upon thousands of males and females who are either dateless or, if they have passed the first hurdle, spending awkward, unhappy and completely unsatisfying evenings with members of the opposite sex.

It needn't be that way for you. It is quite possible for you to have a satisfactory date almost every time you wish one, even if you are not pretty or handsome, brilliant or ravishing, strong and broad or sweet and clinging. If you don't believe it, just look about you and evaluate those who seem to be forever "having a ball." What have they got that you have not? Not a thing. They just happen to know how.

To paraphrase Caesar, all dates are divided into two parts: getting them and living them.

First, then, what is the secret of getting a date? The fundamental error made by members of both sexes is that of underrating themselves and overrating others. Once you permit yourself to think that a girl is too pretty or popular or desirable to go out with you, your inferiority complex will become a badge on your lapel and your approach, if you finally screw up courage to make an approach, will be timid and ineffectual. Once you think a boy is too handsome or smart to bother with you, you may be almost certain he will hardly notice you are alive.

In dating, as in every other phase of our lives, the value we set on ourselves becomes the value others set on us. Who knows better than you whether you are worth going out with? Why should anyone choose to doubt your own measure of your worth?

I do not mean to imply that if you are a rather average person all you have to do to date a movie star or a football hero is to telephone and, exuding confidence in your merit, extend an invitation. I do, however, mean to imply that self-esteem will serve better than anything else in getting you *first* dates with people you have met—people who have actually entered your world—as opposed to the movie star or football hero you may worship from afar but who has little or no knowledge of your existence. Within this limitation, you will probably be amazed at the high caliber of the people who will consider an evening with you well worth while. (I have stressed the word "first" because second and subsequent dates with given individuals depend pretty much on what happens while you are experiencing the first one.)

Indeed, it often happens that one has more success in approaching more desirable or glamorous individuals than in extending invitations to quite ordinary ones. The reason for this is that too many people are self-deprecators and therefore hesitate to aspire too greatly.

Not long ago there was a television discussion group composed of about six of the most beautiful women in the United States. They were all talented, as well, and quite successful in their respective fields. Do you know what several of them considered a major problem in their lives? You guessed it: dating.

Said one, in effect: "I believe men are afraid to ask me out because they think I would refuse an invitation. They think I'm too beautiful and famous and popular either to be free of an evening or, if free, to bother with the likes of them. As a result, I have very few dates, and I often have to initiate the ones I do have."

The same thing may be true, in a more modest way, in your own circle of acquaintances. The very fact that you consider yourself good enough to ask for a date gives you sufficient stature to have your invitation considered respectfully by the most desirable person you know.

Naturally, self-esteem must be backed up by merit, and the purpose of all we have discussed and have still to discuss is the development of a meritorious personality. It is not enough merely to say "I am a worthwhile person." You have to believe it and you *can* believe it if you take the trouble to develop your talents and your manner and your attitudes to the limit of your ability. You and most other people have potential, but potential is inadequate if it is dormant. If you have made the most of yourself, however modestly you may view yourself, you will have self-esteem. Add a bit of nerve and you've got it made.

Since I have promised not to encroach upon the preserves of the newspaper columnists I shall not presume to offer suggestions as to the manner in which an invitation to spend an evening with you should be extended. From coast to coast there are hundreds of such suggestions published daily. For our purposes it is sufficient to point out for emphasis the fact that in the matter of *making* dates it is a man's world while in the matter of *living* them the woman has the upper hand. Since it is better to have no date at all than to have an unsuccessful one, the advantage overall is weighted in the woman's favor, though it must be confessed that not many teen-age girls would agree with this point of view.

In our society the male of the species has a free hand in the making of dates. He can invite a female to a movie, to a lecture, to a concert or even to nothing at all—to a walk or a talk, so to speak. The road is not quite so smooth for the female. The girl who would call a boy with whom she has never been out and say, "Do you want to go to the movies with me Saturday night?" would usually be considered "aggressive." She might be branded a boy-chaser. It isn't fair, it doesn't make sense, but that's the way it is in our part of the world.

On the other hand, it is quite acceptable for her to invite a boy to a preplanned group activity such as a prom, a party, or a club boat ride or picnic. Her success in *living* such a date will decide whether there will be future dates with him and whether after the first time there need be a group activity to make it legal. It may be added parenthetically that a resourceful female can always manage to find a group activity to which to invite a male to whom she is attracted, thus in some measure equalizing the status of the sexes even in this phase of dating.

As the father of daughters, I am aware of the fact that a magic formula for making dates would be much more satisfactory than anything that has been written above. Unfortunately, magic formulas went out with dragons and fairy godmothers. We live in the age of the computer which, despite its great speed of operation, deals only with the natural and eschews the supernatural. Fortunately (as any father knows) the computer accepts as real and natural the law of averages. If you have enough self-esteem to ask for a date and to try again and again if you fail once or twice or three times or more, the law of averages will *inevitably* become effective and a certain proportion of the girls or boys you invite will accept. If you are highly desirable the proportion will be larger than it will be if you are merely average; but even if you are considerably below average you cannot fail to meet with occasional success in overcoming the first hurdle to satisfactory dating: *getting* the date. Again I would ask you to look at some of the boys and girls who have dates and see whether this is not so.

What you *do* with the date after you get it is the big thing. Not only will it decide whether there will be subsequent outings with the same person; it will, if you take the trouble to prepare yourself for it adequately, pave the way for easier dating with others. When boys or girls, men or women, have a good time with members of the opposite sex, it is not their habit to make a secret of the fact. (This is, of course, one of the reasons for making certain that the sort of good time you have is one that you won't be ashamed of having discussed.)

Essentially, there is little difference between the personality requirements for a date and those for living with friends, neighbors, relatives or colleagues. The attributes that make you a desirable companion in one phase of your life are more or less the same as those that make you wanted in another. Where variations may be indicated is in the emphasis you exert. Thus, politeness and good breeding may serve best with casual acquaintances; unselfishness and the willingness to sacrifice with friends; helpfulness with neighbors; congeniality with hosts or guests, and so on.

In dating (though there may be exceptions for certain persons with special and highly exclusive interests) the best attributes to keep on display are these:

1. Lightness.
2. Talkativeness.
3. Agreeableness.
4. Dignity.

Why is a quality which is comparatively so unimportant in other relationships placed at the head of the list in this one? Because (though the fundamental purpose of dating is mating) the conscious reason for dating is the desire to have a good time. We are dealing here with early dating, before Cupid has landed his arrow and legitimized seriousness, planning, deep understanding and even mild quarreling. A boy or a girl who has a good time on a date will seek the company of his or her date again and again. You cannot offer your partner on a date a good time if you start off in a mood of heaviness, sadness, ill temper or worrisomeness.

It is true, of course, that you cannot turn lightness on as you would a water tap. If you have reason for worry or sadness it is difficult if not impossible to hide it sufficiently to appear convincingly carefree. But since the very reason for the date is fun it becomes pointless without fun. More than that, to inflict a heavy evening on another is almost a guarantee that it will be your last evening together.

Do not make or accept early dates at times in your life when you cannot be carefree. If something happens that makes you heavyhearted or angry after you have already made a date, cancel it; you can do this gently and politely without hurting your partner as much as you would by spending an unenjoyable evening with him. If it is too late to cancel, explain the situation frankly at the beginning of the evening; in this way your partner will be reassured that it is through no fault of his that you cannot be light and gay.

Young people—and they are the ones who, because of lack of experience, have the most difficulty with dating—

are lucky enough to be the ones who most infrequently have cause for serious sadness or worry, so for them, at least, the necessity for avoiding dates for such a reason should not constitute more than an occasional problem.

In the early stages of the male-female relationships lightness of spirit can actually bring magic back into the age of the computer. When you walk together in this spirit, the most commonplace things become wonderful. The people you pass, the moon in the sky, the bump in the sidewalk, the music of the band, the chance touch of hands, even the pouring rain, become cause for laughter, thrill, secret understanding, anticipation, wonder and happiness. It is nature's way with a boy and a girl, but you have to give nature an assist by entering the scene in a mood of lightness.

But a light mood dies swiftly in the presence of a tied tongue. You may spend hours of bliss with a sweetheart or a spouse without once saying a word, but silence on an early date is catastrophic. And so talkativeness, often an undesirable attribute, becomes in this aspect of your life a *sine qua non*.

Between a boy and a girl on a date there is often a natural embarrassment. Though consciously they are merely spending an evening together to have fun, they know unconsciously that the mating reason is the real one. In our society, despite all of the new freedom of sex discussion that is apparent, the average young male and female together on a date for the first couple of times are in a process of exploration. Neither will admit to the other at this point that anything more than fun is involved. Talk is a diversion from the main theme and each welcomes talk from the other. Talk puts both at ease.

Oh, you may say, that sort of thinking is for squares. Nowadays boys and girls are extremely sophisticated. They know the score. Many of them are quite conscious of nature's plan and they don't have to kid themselves or others by beating about the bush with diversionary talk. As a matter of fact, sex experience is not uncommon even on first or second dates.

That could be true, though I doubt that there is as much sex on real dates as there is in magazine stories and sex surveys about real dates. The fact remains that advice on dating is avidly sought by millions upon millions of young folk who would not need such advice if there were as much loose sexual intercourse as the writers and pollsters would have us believe. Any girl knows that if she is prepared to go all the way she can get all the dates she wants without anyone's advice.

However, even if the writers and surveyors were correct there would be no really satisfactory dates without talkativeness, for the natural embarrassment to which I, as a square, referred to above is not, by far, the only reason for the importance of an untied tongue. This is apart from the self-evident fact that there can be no genuine joy or satisfaction for the girl who can get dates easily only because she is prepared to sacrifice herself as an instrument for a boy's brief physical satisfaction; or for the boy who has to spend hours of boredom with a girl whom he has dated for that brief satisfaction alone.

Good talk on a date has value for its own sake: it is of itself a source of fun and enjoyment. Talk breaks the ice better than anything else, and puts both partners at ease. Talk develops mutual understanding of dreams, goals, attitudes, agreements and disagreements. Good talk has a longer-lasting magnetic effect on the date-partner than sex without commitment, than prettiness or handsomeness, or than lavish spending.

Can you be talkative on a date? You certainly can, even if you don't do more than a tenth of the talking. Talkativeness as it is meant here means anything that will keep the conversation from lagging. In all fairness, you would not want to monopolize the conversation in any event.

Good talk includes good listening; it stimulates good talk by the partner as well. Therefore the most fruitful opening to an evening of good talk is a question. Countless casual dates have been transformed into "going steady" as a result of the fact that one or another of the partners had the good sense to know that the most stimulating phrases in the language are "What do you think of . . . ?" and "How do you like . . . ?" It is not suggested that you limit your contribution to questions. You must have opinions and knowledge and banter of your own to offer. In Chapter Twelve you will find a suggested approach to the development of your conversational ability.

I recall vividly an incident that illustrates better than

any analytical discussion the importance attached to conversation by intelligent and desirable young people. It happened by chance that I was driving by the home of a friend I had not seen in several years. I decided to stop off and say hello. My friend and his wife greeted me warmly and introduced me to two college boys who had come to take their daughter and one of her girl friends out to the movies. The girls were upstairs "putting their faces on" as my friend's wife expressed it.

It was just about the time of the most intensive phase of the Presidential election campaign and we all got into a quiet debate about the issues. About ten minutes later the girls came down. The faces they had put on were lovely, and their figures were, as the saying goes, something. My friend's daughter smiled to me in greeting and introduced her pretty friend. The boys, warming up to the debate, scarcely noticed the girls.

Another ten minutes went by and we all remained deeply absorbed in our conversation. All, that is, except the two girls, who contributed not a word and who fidgeted impatiently. Finally one of the girls said, "We'd better hurry or we'll be late." The boy with whom she was to be paired nodded and said, "We'll only be another minute." The minute stretched to five, and to save the situation I said that I would have to leave. The boys reluctantly terminated the debate and started off with the girls.

It was very clear to me that if these college boys had had anything to look forward to that evening beyond the prettiness of their companions they would have left with them many minutes earlier. They were obviously starved for good talk and, just as obviously, they knew there would be none of it for the rest of the evening. Had the girls been plain Janes with something to say, the boys would have been much more eager to start the date. Pretty faces, and even lovemaking, cannot satisfy hour after hour and date after date. Human beings require mental stimulation when they themselves have mental alertness.

As I have indicated, the third thing you should bring along with you on your date is agreeableness. Come prepared to be flexible: about what you will do together, about the subjects of conversation, about when to call it a night and the like. Two people on a date should defer to each other's wishes in these matters. This does not mean that you should spend all your time saying "After you, Gaston," because if both partners are totally wishy-washy nothing will get done or said. It is, nevertheless, better to yield than to be stubborn. It is possible to carry your point and lose the possibility of another date. When the goal is fun, having your own way becomes a Pyrrhic victory.

There is a middle way. If you have a preference, express it quickly. Usually your partner will go along. If he demurs, yield. If he is consistently mulish, keep yielding and count the evening lost. You won't want to go out with him again anyway. Most of the time there will be a fair give and take that will help you both to have a good time and make you look forward to a repeat performance.

The ideal date, the one most likely to lead to other dates, is one in which both partners are light of spirit, pleasantly quick of tongue and agreeably considerate. If only one of the partners—you—contributes all three attitudes at the beginning, the other will soon be swept along in the same way and a good time will be guaranteed.

We now have left the fourth ingredient—dignity. Dignity is difficult to describe and even more difficult to instill. It is one of those attributes that you either have or have not.

Dignity is that quality without which no other quality or combination of qualities can gain respect for you; and if your dating period is to lead to its ultimate goal, marriage with your very best date, the maintenance of your dignity is utterly essential.

Dignity is the refusal to permit any other human being to do to you or with you that which will lower your self-esteem and to do nothing yourself that will have the same effect; for, as we have said more than once, you will be measured always by your own measure of yourself. Dignity eschews crudity, boorishness, cheapness, dishonesty, spinelessness and meanness.

In a sense, dignity involves the drawing of a line that says "Thus far and no farther." The line can be drawn against the mauling of your person and easy sex; against disrespectful talk; against impoliteness; against advantage-taking; against gross unpunctuality; or against any action that is careless of your worth or your feelings.

You should do your share to make your date a happy and successful one, but if your lightness of spirit is repaid with sullenness, or your readiness to talk with glum silence, or your agreeableness with disagreeableness, you will, and rightly, lose the respect of your partner and further dates will have no value for you. If your partner makes it clear that you are being used for your money or your body or merely as a stopgap in the absence of a preferred partner, your dignity demands that you either set the other straight or call a halt at once, even if it means breaking off the date smack in the middle.

Maintaining your dignity is a perfectly safe procedure. You simply cannot lose. The worst that can happen is the best that can happen: you will be forced to date only with people who respect themselves as you respect yourself.

We move on now to a less happy phase of the male-female relationship with the hope that it is not and never will be of direct personal interest to you.

Chapter Nine

WHAT TO DO WHEN CUPID GOES

❦ "An outstanding feature of the heart as a machine is its capacity to perform continuous work, for it beats continuously during the life of the body. In the case of the human heart, this contracts 100,000 times a day. . . . Another remarkable feature is the reserve power of the heart."—*Encyclopaedia Britannica.*

The staid editors of *Britannica,* who know all about everything from Aabenraa in Denmark to the Zygote, or fertilized egg, know all about the human heart . . . all except one thing: that a heart can break without physical cause and that it can be mended without the services of a physician.

Nevertheless, it is often encouraging to remember what these editors have to say about the endurance of the heart, and its reserve power. When Cupid has fled the coop, so to speak, there is comfort in the knowledge that the heart he has left aching so miserably will continue to do its job until the pain has eased. Any organ that can stay on the job, day and night, through good times and bad, as the heart does, can be counted upon to survive the medically nonexistent break that Cupid all too often inflicts on the victims of his imperfection in the art of love.

While we are absorbed in this highly scientific discussion, it may be fruitful to quote a heart specialist of the seventeenth century, one François de La Rochefoucauld who, among his numerous appellations, was known as France's greatest coiner of maxims. Said this sage: "When the heart is still agitated by the remains of a passion, we are more ready to receive a new one than when we are entirely cured." In the prosaic language of the space age we call this falling on the rebound.

All of this may sound rather cruel and callous to one who has only recently experienced a love-life crisis—a taking-lightly of a form of unhappiness that is as tragic as it is real. Unfortunately—perhaps fortunately—that's how people are. Find yourself the victim of a coronary thrombosis or of the flu and everyone around you becomes filled with deep and genuine concern. Break a leg and everyone and his cousin will help you across the street as long as you wear a cast. But weep as you will inside over a lost love and all you will get is an almost ghoulish ribbing or, at best, the well-meant advice to snap out of it. This even from people who have been through it themselves. "In normal mental health," they will tell you, "a broken heart takes at the most a year to mend." Perhaps they are right; the experience of the world seems to bear out their contention. Yet I am inclined to sympathize with the comment of one young man who had recently been jilted: "A hell of a lot of good that does me NOW!"

But consider. Would it be better for the lovelorn if all of the people in their lives joined them in their weeping? Even in cases of physical accident or breakdown the least helpful friends are those who wring their hands and moan along with the victims. To cite an extreme illustration, I know of one man who was blinded in his thirtieth year and who was the recipient of the most tremendous amount of sympathy and help you could imagine. Yet, after one year of darkness he was in total despair and on the verge of suicide. Today he is a well-adjusted, productive and creative member of his family and of society, not as happy as he would be if he could see, of course, but far more happy than he had ever dreamed possible in those early days of his affliction. What turned the tide? An apparently merciless scolding by a friend who loved him so that he could not bear to see him in such a low state.

If you have broken off with a sweetheart or if you have been parted from a spouse, you need advice more than you need sympathy, not because sympathy will harm you or because advice will help you at the time, but because it is true that broken hearts mend and when they do mend it is better for you if you have followed good advice even mechanically and without your heart in the process. We shall try in the following pages to offer some good advice to those who have had their love dreams shattered.

The very first fact to etch into your brain is this: every person alive has troubles of his own, and to each person his own troubles are of the most immediate concern. (You will recall that this volume is not being written for saints.) He may sympathize with your worries for a while—perhaps for a long while—but he will not forever carry the burdens of your sadness. Sooner or later everyone reaches a saturation point, and at that point you become an undesirable problem—a nuisance, if you will. People who clucked sympathetically and patted your shoulder every time you unfolded your tale of woe will start avoiding you. They will not invite you to social gatherings: "I'd like to ask Susan but she puts such a damper on everything." They will pretend not to see you when they pass you by: "Lord, if I say hello, Joe will start filling my ear with that heartbreak stuff."

Then, when the day comes—and come it will—when you awaken and hear the birds chirping and see the sun streaming into your room and breathe deep and realize suddenly that at last you are free of heartbreak, you will find yourself out of the swim of social living and practically alone in the world.

The second fact to learn well is this: It will take longer for the break to mend if you isolate yourself from the world with your sorrow; and when at last the break *does* mend you will be equally out of touch with the world of people.

Obviously, the correct course to follow is to go along outwardly as though nothing has happened. (This cannot be done in divorce situations, but at this point we are concentrating upon sweetheart disasters.) This is the most difficult course to follow and in the beginning by far the most painful. Susan, after parting from her loved one, will be more unhappy on a date with a new boy than she would be alone in her room, weeping over the picture of the estranged one. She will be making odious comparisons, she will be saying to herself, "Maybe this is all just a bad dream," and she will be exhausted with the effort to maintain a conversation in which she has not the slightest interest. Joe, who has been jilted, will have the same problems if he tries dating other girls, as he should.

In the office, at the homes of friends, on theatre parties and excursions—everywhere and all the time it will be like that: a going through the motions without interest or desire and with an aching emptiness inside; always acting a part, never really living. But that is what must be done to avoid damage to the personality; once your friends and relatives start seeing you as a hermit, or a problem or a nuisance and a bother, it becomes exceedingly difficult for them to see you in another light at a later time when, whatever you may think today, you will desperately want them to.

You have read tales of actors and actresses who, in the face of private tragedy, go on in their roles as happy, carefree or even comic personalities. Granted you may not be of equal Thespian talent. You can, however, go on with the show to the best of your ability. Even if your acting falls short of brilliance, it will serve you better than carrying a torch around with you all the time or burying yourself away from the world. In any event, what is required more than talent is determination, common sense and intestinal fortitude. You have common sense or you wouldn't be seeking advice. Try to develop the determination and the intestinal fortitude.

By one of those freaks of circumstance, the very heartbreak that can destroy your personality if you deal with it unintelligently can serve to make you a warmer, more generous, more tolerant and more attractive personality if you take advantage of your common sense. It has been said that he cannot be supremely happy who has never been unutterably sad; that the physician should first cure himself; that one who has not known want cannot appreciate plenty. The psychoanalyst who has problems of his own has greater insight, as a result, into the problems of his patients.

People in love for the first time are notoriously self-centered; even their obsession with their sweethearts is a form of self-gratification. The same people, once they have loved and lost, once they have recovered from the loss sufficiently to function normally, invariably develop a more sympathetic, more understanding and more tolerant attitude toward the general run of humanity. Instinctively they understand that they have shared an emotional earthquake with many thousands of others and they draw closer in spirit to the others, as we all do when we have an experience in common. This new outlook is evident in their manner, in their voices, in their general attitudes. To their personalities has been added the ingredient of insight, than which there is no greater personality treasure. You can lack almost any other personality trait or traits . . . when people know you *understand* them, they are drawn to you.

If, however, you repulse all your friends by incorrect surface attitudes before you recover from your heartbreak, you will lose not only your friends but the entire opportunity to benefit from the mellowing influence of suffering.

So: if you have loved and lost, become an actor. In the words of another song, "Smile though your heart may be breaking." We are peculiar creatures with great limitations. It is almost impossible for us to do two things at once, to have two thoughts at the same time, to have our faces contradict our thoughts. Almost impossible but not quite impossible. We can, for instance, force our lips to curve upward in a smile when we are unhappy, but the very act of compulsion creates a modifying impact on each gesture or thought: the smile becomes something less than a spontaneous smile but the unhappiness is watered down somewhat. Two things, each done perfectly or very well when done alone, will be less perfect or less well done when done in conjunction. You may be a fine penman and a good pianist, but if you try writing a letter with one hand and playing the piano with the other at the same time, your letter will be an almost unintelligible scrawl and your playing will win you no applause.

When the two things you are doing are in different areas—that is to say when one is physical and the other mental or spiritual—the physical act always achieves predominance over the long haul; in the final stage, the physical act conquers the mental and the spiritual and casts it out, substituting a mental or spiritual attitude that conforms to the physical act. As a wild example take a man who thinks noble thoughts with his mind and steals and kills with his hands. If he persists in stealing and killing, his thoughts must necessarily turn from noble to brutal. If the situation were reversed and he thought only ugly thoughts but did only kindly deeds, his thoughts would eventually have to become kindly, for the influence of his physical acts would have to prevail. We can force ourselves to take physical action but we cannot force the trend of our thoughts.

Therefore, if you compel yourself to live a normal life and follow a normal routine when your heart is broken, you will find, sooner or later, that your thoughts will not be able to divorce themselves from the actuality of your physical actions. In the process of forcing conversation you must take at least a part of your mind away from your sorrow. The same holds true in the process of forcing yourself to dress well, to look well, to go places, to see things. Eventually the habit pattern you impose on your body and on your actions will impose itself on your mind and heart as well and you will be cured without having lost a friend.

The third fact of life that you must learn is this: you

will love again. It may even come to pass that in curing your broken heart you will discover that what you have lost is not only not irreplaceable but that it might conceivably be replaced with something even more desirable.

This should be a consoling thought but it must be said at the same time that there is a sort of danger in the situation. At the beginning of the chapter we recorded the words of La Rochefoucauld: "When the heart is still agitated by the remains of a passion, we are more ready to receive a new one than when we are entirely cured." More survivors of broken engagements marry on the rebound than is good for the institution of marriage.

Suppose Susan, who has broken her engagement, should chance to date with Joe, who has been jilted. This would be in accord with the best advice of the present writer. But suppose, further, that during the course of the evening they find out about each other's heartbreak and get to talking about it. They would have so much in common and would be so understanding of each other's woe that a close bond of kinship would be quickly established. Both are blue, both are lonely and both, still under the glow of the love that was gone, would begin to weave a spell under which they would confuse the glow with the person and begin to imagine, by a process of transference, that they were in love with each other though nothing could be further from the truth.

Still transposing the newfound friend for the lost love they rush into marriage, as so often happens, only to come to their senses a short time later with the knowledge that they have married as complete strangers who are not even in love. Marriage on the rebound could conceivably be successful, but in the nature of things and people as they are, the mathematical odds against such good fortune are great.

A common sense rule of thumb, then, would be: do not make an avowal of love or a commitment of marriage after a broken love affair until at least six months have gone by and until you have known the new person for at least six months. A year would be better, but who wants to slow the footsteps of Eros?

If yours is a case of divorce rather than the breaking of an engagement or a jilting, your heartbreak may not be quite so painful as that of the never-wed young lovers. Divorce is usually the final act after a long peiod of suffering in which two people become so incompatible that the only thing that can relieve their pain is separation. On the other hand, your social problem may be greater. You would appear to your friends and acquaintances to be slightly moronic if you pretended that nothing had happened and went about your business as before.

There are, of course, certain aspects of your situation that call for the same precautions as those advocated above. People do get just as tired of divorced persons who keep harping on the subject of their woes as they do o the weeping girl who has broken her engagement; and you can lose just as much as the girl would lose by withdrawing into isolation. You and the disengaged girl are entitled to a brief period of sympathy and consultation but as soon as possible you must get off other people's backs.

For you, too, there are a few facts of life that properly learned will ease your way.

The first of these is the fact that the breakup of your marriage may be the biggest thing in your life but it is only a nine-days' wonder to the rest of the world. In the beginning, every time your friends see you they will say to themselves, "Poor Jennie (or poor Jack), what a pity." But after a while they will say to themselves merely, "Oh, here's Jennie (or Jack)." If you keep on imagining that for months and months and years and years everyone you know will have your divorce pop into his mind the moment he sees you, you are more egotistical than wise.

Of course, you've got to give them some help, at least in the beginning. Without talking about it obsessively, you must make it clear that you are not embarrassed by the mention of it and that you are not hiding the truth in a closet like a skeleton. They should know that it is not required of them that in conversations in your presence they must avoid any discussion that might be in some way tied up in the minds of others with your status. They should feel free, if they wish, to tell anyone about it, in your presence and in your absence. It should not be made a possible source of embarrassment to them.

The second vital fact is this: practically all married women are matchmakers at heart. Whatever their psychological motivations, they seem to be unable to tolerate the existence of an eligible male or female on the loose,

most particularly one who has been divorced. How helpful this can be to you can be gathered from what follows.

Married couples customarily associate with other married couples. A divorce in a given social circle could,
therefore, create an immediate difficulty: what do you do
with an odd man or woman at a party, at a dinner, at the
theatre or on a group trip? For the odd man or woman,
there could be discomfort in the knowledge that he or she,
once an integral part of the group, has now become a
problem child—a sort of fifth wheel. Even if they all tried
to go along as before, the unattached person would stand
out like a sore thumb among all the mated ones.

I say such problems "could" arise. Normally, because
married women are constituted as they are, they rarely do
arise. After what they consider a decent interval, these
women start casting about for potential mates for their
divorced friends. You will find yourself being invited subtly or unsubtly to meet someone at a party or other social
event. The first time this happens, and as often thereafter
as you wish, your acceptance of the invitation should be
prompt and enthusiastic. After all, you don't have to marry
or even date everyone you are introduced to, but the fact
that for that evening, at least, you are coupled with someone will put the whole party at ease and prevent the establishment of a mental image of yourself as a problem.

There is, of course, another side to the entertainment
coin. As a married person, you not only visited others
but invited others to visit with you and, if you are like
most of us, your friends were married couples. What do

you do now that you are no longer married? Do you discard your old married friends and seek out new unmarried ones? Do you begin to associate only with divorced people? Or do you continue to invite the same people who always came to your home?

Here is what one thirty-five-year-old divorcee told me of her own very successful experience:

"At first I didn't want to go anywhere or have anyone come to see me. I had all of the mental blocks you could think of. After a while, though, I realized that I was being foolish. As I thought about the matter I began to see something I had never thought of: though a broken marriage is a tragic thing and should be avoided if at all possible, the new situation did offer me a certain amount of choice and freedom that I had almost forgotten about in ten years of marriage. Don't get me wrong—that kind of freedom is no substitute for the chains of matrimony, and the fact that I have remarried is an indication of how I feel about it. Nevertheless, in my low state of mind, it was a plus.

"I didn't give up my old friends but I began to mix them a little more with unmarried people. I found that married and unmarried people mix very well if you steer the conversation away from children and I never did care very much about the ones who couldn't speak of anything else. Sometimes I had a group of only unmarried people over and you'd be amazed at how much I had in common with them after only a short time of singleness. The problems of shopping alone were fascinating. I found that the whole world is geared to married people—half of every loaf of bread has to be thrown away because it goes stale before one person can finish it; half of every can of soup is wasted or at best not as good as the first half if consumed the next day; the small-quantity purchaser takes second place in the store to the family shopper; people look at you queerly if you invite a person of the opposite sex to your apartment—I could go on and on.

"Whenever I discovered an advantage in the single state, that, too, served to stimulate discussion. Did you know, by the way, that it's almost always possible to get a single seat at a theatre even when the show is a hit? The trouble is, who wants to go to the theatre alone? What I'm trying to show is that I found myself beginning to 'fit in' more with more different kinds of people and I made the most of it. How do you think I found my wonderful new husband? In my own living room it was. Since couples were no longer strictly required at my home, I said 'Bring him along' when one of our old married couples called one day to tell me they couldn't make a dinner appointment because a friend from the Midwest had dropped in.

"He was a bachelor, one of the confirmed sort. I told him I didn't blame him for being so confirmed, because he could always get a single seat at the theatre, could snore all he wanted to, could live in a filthy house if he felt like it, could go to the hospital every time he got the flu and not be bothered by a wife fussing and bothering all over the place and could do all of the other wonderful things I had on my list. I promise you I was only trying to be funny but the next thing he said was, 'My God, you paint a horrible picture. Will you come with me if I get two single seats at the theatre for Wednesday evening?'

"I'm sure you think what I'm saying is silly but it really isn't. It's just another way of saying that if a person *has* to part from a husband she should not only look at the dark side—and I admit there is a very dark side—but at the new worlds that open up. I don't know how to express it, but through these new worlds I found the way back to the old world, which for me was the best kind. Anyhow, I didn't mope."

I guess she *is* a little mixed up, but in a delightful way and I can't express her philosophy more competently. One thing bears no contradiction: she did not permit the tragedy of divorce to warp her personality. Rather, she managed to extract from the experience a little something that enriched her personality, as every experience can do for people who stand up to the winds of life instead of being uprooted.

Chapter Ten

GIVE YOURSELF AWAY

❧ The advice to give yourself away is not intended to mean that you should be careless about revealing your hand in a poker game or, if you are a young lady, that you should be casual about your virtue. We have become so accustomed to colloquialisms that too often we forget the literal meanings of words, and we find it necessary to make explanatory comments like "I meant exactly what I said." In this book, to give yourself away means "exactly what I said"—to give *yourself* away.

In the preceding pages we gave some attention to the merits of sharing: sharing your apartment, sharing your experiences, sharing a measure of your material assets and even sharing your loneliness. But the biggest and best thing you can share is yourself, and the more of yourself you give away the more attractive you will become in the eyes of those who know you and in your own eyes. We touched on this very briefly in Chapter Three.

The world is divided into groups in every area of human interest or endeavor that you can think of. In the area we are about to explore there are two groups: those who recognize a wrong, or an injustice, or a misfortune and cry out bitterly, "Somebody ought to do something about this"; and those who, recognizing the same wrong or injustice or misfortune, cast about for ways and means of setting things right. The future of mankind rests in the hands of the latter group, which is made up of those precious souls who are prepared to give themselves wholeheartedly and unreservedly to the causes and crusades in which they believe.

Sometimes it takes courage, for the cause or crusade may not be popular. Sometimes it takes selflessness, for the cause or crusade may be supremely demanding. Sometimes it takes determination, for the cause or crusade may present many obstacles. And sometimes all it takes is a love of mankind and the willingness to demonstrate the love with deeds and action. Courage, determination, selflessness, love—whatever the motivation for giving yourself away it will make its impact on your personality image, for the world will see and recognize it and you yourself will be completely aware of it.

You give one or more of these and you receive . . . fulfillment, than which there is no more satisfying gift. Fulfillment is the one thing all men seek and few men find. Some of the few find it in creative work, some in rearing families, some in religion. But see: even these find it by giving themselves unreservedly away. On the other hand, the vast majority of us have no great talent and all too many of us go to work every day to make a living and not for the love of our work; children grow up and depart from the nest, and parents who found their fulfillment in them are left with a void; and as for religion, what is it for those who really understand its meaning but faith and the call to help their fellow men? You will find all truly religious people in the vanguard of the causes and crusades with which we are now concerning ourselves.

Fulfillment is there for the taking if only we understand it. If there is a wrong you would like to see righted, if there is a hurt that you can heal, if there is a truth you think the world should know—don't just stand there. Do something! The moment you start you will feel yourself spiritually, emotionally and mentally enriched; and when you become so wrapped up in the cause that you are actually giving yourself to it, fulfillment will be yours. A man fulfilled is a man whole, and a whole man radiates his completeness. His personality glows. His presence is meaningful. It *must* be so, else why would the urge to fulfillment be so dominant?

"A very nice sermon," I can hear you saying. "Very inspiring. But frankly, I didn't come here to be preached to or to be inspired. I came for some practical advice. What do you want me to do—go out with my sword and kill dragons who are preying on beautiful princesses? Shall I take my seventy-five dollars a week and feed all the poor people? Shall I stride into City Hall and tell the elected officials that they had better do their duty and give us clean government, or else? You see what I mean? I don't have any 'or else.' I'm just one person. The world has been here for a long time and all of these hurts and injustices you are talking about have very deep roots—my arms aren't strong enough to pull the roots out."

Right you are.

Fortunately for you, we have already agreed that we are neither saints nor geniuses, so nobody expects us to give away our seventy-five dollars a week or to cure the ills of the world all by ourselves or to pull out the deep roots without help. But think: if you got seventy-five people to give away a dollar a week that they hadn't been giving away, the good would be as great as though you yourself had given all the money. And if you got a man with a truck to tie a rope to the roots and to the truck, all he would have to do is step on the gas and up would come the roots.

No, not having any "or else" or not being strong enough to pull up the roots all by yourself is not a problem. What *would* be a problem would be to find something worth doing in the world that you would *have* to do all by yourself . . . or even something that you would be *permitted* to do all by yourself. Smart as you may be, the chances are that you could not think of a reasonably important cause or crusade that someone else had not already thought of and done something about.

Despite the fact that there are so many, many people

who go along from one day to the next without ever giving a thought to anything but their own personal satisfactions, there are still enough people who dare, persist, sacrifice and love enough to "do something about it" to cause such a proliferation of organizations dedicated to good works that *choosing* one or several in which to enlist poses far greater difficulty than *finding* them. Name a disease that afflicts mankind; there is an organization dedicated to its eradication. Think of a religion; there is an organization (sometimes many organizations) concerned with the welfare of its more unfortunate members. Conjure up an ideology, an educational problem, a public need—there are organizations galore working on them. Problems of age, of youth, of crime, of poverty, of economics, of traffic, of air pollution, of food purity, of cruelty to animals or children, of domestic and conjugal life, of slums, of addiction to drugs or alcohol, of mental adjustment, of public safety, of war and peace, of labor, of management and hundreds more, all are being examined, explored, analyzed and coped with by groups and organizations composed of dedicated men and women who are finding fulfillment as an unexpected by-product of their willingness to "do something about it." As for you, there is no harm or discredit to you if you *consciously* seek fulfillment in this manner, provided only that you don't expect it to come out of participation in a cause or a crusade in which you have no strong emotional involvement. To be fulfilled, you have to do something your heart, not your mind, tells you to do.

Having myself been involved, emotionally and pro-
fessionally, in a number of causes, I am familiar with
literally scores of cases in which persons who before their
own involvement in these causes were living unsatisfac-
tory, empty and boring lives—persons who were unknown,
unsung and unloved beyond their own immediate circle
of friends and relatives—and who suddenly found new
zest, recognition, satisfaction, joy, insight and often, believe it or not, career advancement after their involvement.

Here we can observe only a few of them but these will
be sufficient to tell the whole story and point the way for
you. First comes Mr. Herbert Conover, a self-made businessman. After Mr. Conover had finished the job of
making himself, he discovered, to his great surprise and
disappointment, that he had done a pretty poor job of it.
He had a good, thriving business, plenty of money, an attractive wife, and two bright sons in college; moreover, he
had his health intact. What more could he ask of life? He
asked one thing: acceptance of himself. Without it he
found little satisfaction in anything else.

You see, he had given himself (yes, given himself—and
while he was giving himself his life was zestful and he had
no self-doubts) so completely to the cause of making himself a successful businessman that he had had no time for
any other form of character or personality development.
He had read no books, listened to no music, failed to keep
up with the crosscurrents of contemporary history beyond
those of commerce and the stock market, and acquired no

social grace. When his job was done and he no longer had to give himself to it, he was lost in a strange world that nodded politely when he passed by but did not take him to its bosom. His wife loved him, but while he had been busy giving himself to himself she had passed him by. In his frequent absences "on business" she had been compelled to occupy her time with matters in which he had had no part. She had taken courses in appreciation of art and literature; she had become active in a charitable organization and in civic work; she had read voraciously and she had made many friends with whom she engaged regularly in sparkling conversation. Now they had little in common except routine family problems.

His sons loved him too; but they were college men and he and they spoke no common language. His business associates were ready to talk business with him, but after thirty years of business talk he had had enough. Business talk bored him and there was nothing else he could talk about.

He toyed with the idea of going to night school but he did not go. He tried concerts but they had no meaning for him. He opened a book or two but closed them as quickly as he had opened them. He was lost and miserable. Now he accompanied his wife to parties, but while she chattered with her friends he sat silent and glum; he did not even know what they were talking about. He was not a stupid man, just an incomplete one. There seemed to be nothing he really wanted to do. All of his efforts to improve himself failed because they came from the mind and not from the heart.

One day his wife, who saw and sympathized with his plight, attempted to interest him with a story about a neighbor's child who was mentally retarded. "You have no idea," she said, "how that little girl's parents suffer. How lucky we are to have such healthy and well-adjusted children."

"Isn't there anything they can do?" he asked, his compassion aroused. "Do they need help to pay for doctors? I'd be glad to do something for them."

"No," said his wife. "They have enough money. The doctors just don't seem to be able to do anything."

The remark made him bristle. As a self-made businessman he had not been tolerant of failure. His motto had been "You can do anything if you really want to and if you try hard enough." He pondered for a moment, then said, "That's nonsense. There ought to be a way to lick that sickness. They've licked tougher ones. I've got a good mind to—"

"To what?" asked his wife.

"To take a big chunk of money and finance a few doctors to do some research—a crash program. I'll bet if they had nothing to do but that, they would come up with something."

Mrs. Conover smiled. "They already have a crash program," she said. "There is an organization that does nothing but raise money for research in behalf of mentally retarded children. They are making progress but they haven't solved the problem yet. For one thing, they don't have enough money. You might give them a contribution."

The next day Mr. Conover visited the offices of the organization and contributed a thousand dollars to its work. In talking to the professional staff member who received his check, he learned that they were short not only on funds but manpower, particularly manpower of leadership caliber. He found himself growing angry. The staff member showed him pictures of retarded children and told him a few very sad tales about some of them. "How can anyone refuse to help these kids?" he demanded.

The staff worker looked at him squarely. "We're very grateful for your donation, Mr. Conover," he said, "but in all fairness, this work has been going on for some time now and this is your first offer to help."

"Well," said Mr. Conover defensively, "I never knew about it before."

"We do a great deal of publicity," said the staff member, "but I guess a lot of people are too busy to read it. There are many who don't know about our work."

Mr. Conover was now emotionally involved. "I promise you one thing," he said, "everybody I know will hear about it very soon. And what's more, I'll get money out of them. I'd like to see anyone turn me down in a thing like this."

That very day he set about visiting his business acquaintances and telling the story of the retarded children. He obtained a number of contributions and brought them back to the office of the organization with a greater sense of satisfaction than he had felt in many months. He did it again the next day and the next. His efforts attracted the attention of the executive director of the organization, who introduced him to several of the volunteer officers, most of whom were businessmen like himself or members of the professions. Before he left them he had accepted the title of campaign chairman of the industry in which he had made his success, with the task of organizing the industry in a drive for funds for mentally retarded children. He carried his responsibility forward with such vigor and dedication that at year's end the total of contributions in his division was proportionately greater than that of any other industrial group in his city.

He was then promoted to the chairmanship of industries, with responsibility for leadership enrollment and campaign results on an inter-industry basis. The more he worked, the more he loved the work. Progress was being made and children were being helped in a way that at one time would have been impossible. The knowledge that this was partly due to his own labors gave him deep and abiding satisfaction.

All this would have been enough for Mr. Conover, even without the acceptance he had yearned for. But something else was happening. As organizations do, this organization publicized his campaign achievements in the newspapers and on radio and television. He became identified in the minds of many people—even people he did not know—as a benefactor of children. When he visited an office to ask for a contribution he often found resistance, but he always found respect and admiration. His neighbors, who had earlier merely nodded and walked swiftly by when they saw him, now sought the privilege of shaking his hand and having him at their homes as a guest. His wife was proud of him and listened endlessly to his recital of campaign problems and achievements. His children began to see him not only with love but with admiration.

When a man is doing good in the world the world is satisfied with him and accepts him as a valued member of society, even if he cannot read or write, even if he is dull at a party, even if music and art are Greek to him.

But let's take another case. Not everyone can have the drive and effectiveness that were demonstrated by Mr. Conover. Some people remain workers in the ranks rather than leaders. Many can work a lifetime for a cause and never get their names in the papers. What of them? Well, there was Gladys Brand, a spinster filing clerk, known to the girls at the office as Miss Nobody, often with the accent on the first word. Of course they never called her that in her hearing, but she knew from their indifference how little they cared about her. It wasn't that they disliked her; she might have preferred something as positive as that. It was their *unawareness* of her that made her unhappy.

Gladys didn't blame people for being indifferent to her. The fact was that she was her own most severe judge. "What should I expect?" she would ask herself. "I'm not pretty, I'm not bright, I'm shy and I lose my tongue, I don't do or say anything exciting. Why should anyone bother with me?"

One day a new girl was hired for the office, Sara Locke by name. Sara didn't know that Gladys was not worth noticing. All she saw was another human being. After several attempts at drawing Gladys into conversation, however, the new girl snapped: "Well, if you're too stuck-up to talk, pardon me for living." To her amazement Gladys burst into tears. "For goodness' sake," said Sara. "What'd I do?"

For perhaps the first time in her life Gladys poured out to another the story of her frustrations and her unhappiness. Sara listened sympathetically and then said, "What you need is an outlet."

"What do you mean?" asked Gladys.

"I mean that you should find something to do that will take you out of yourself and make you stop feeling so sorry for yourself. There are millions of people in the world who would consider themselves to be very lucky to be in your shoes. The sick people, the handicapped, the very poor, the hunted, the unjustly imprisoned—oh, I could name a dozen others. Instead of worrying about yourself so much, why don't you go out and help someone worse off than you are?"

Gladys saw the point and decided to take the advice. At this stage she was being completely selfish. She was looking for an outlet for *herself*, for the purpose of solving her *own* problem. She had no intention of giving herself away. It might be said, indeed, that she was out to get something from people who had less than she had. If that attitude had been maintained she would have failed utterly in achieving her purpose. But since rules are rules only by virtue of exceptions, what started out to be for Gladys a self-serving activity ended by becoming far more than that, though it did serve her well.

Being so shy and hesitant, Gladys was not able to solicit contributions for a worthy cause. She tried once or twice, but her approach was so nebulous and unconvincing that she drew a blank. Neither could she make speeches or enlist the help of others. She offered to address envelopes for a philanthropic organization devoted to aiding the blind and her offer was accepted. Two evenings a week were devoted to this task and she found it merely an extension of her work at the office. The other volunteers soon learned to ignore her in much the same way as she was ignored at her regular job.

She was about to call it quits when she overheard one end of a conversation on the telephone while she was addressing envelopes. "I'm sorry," said a voice, "we don't have a soul here tonight to send out to read. I can't understand it. We get all the help we need for other things, but when it comes to visiting a hospital or a home to read to a blind person we never get enough."

Summoning all of her limited boldness, Gladys approached the telephoner. "I—I'd be glad to go out to read," she said.

At that moment Gladys started a new life. As a sighted person she found that she had untold wealth to give to those who were unsighted. Into the life of a blind man or woman or child she could bring the beauty of the sun and the sky and the flowers, the thrill of adventure, the vision of strange lands and peoples, the drama of great loves. And the more she gave, the more she received. The odd thing was that she no longer cared about her own feelings; she was far more concerned for the happiness of those she served. Some were learning to read for themselves through the Braille method and instead of being disappointed when they no longer needed her, she gloried in their emancipation, as a good mother delights in the growing up to independence of her children.

Hardly anyone other than her wards knew what Gladys was doing. She never saw her name in the papers. For a while she did not even tell anyone about it for fear she would appear to be boasting. And yet a revolution took place in her life. Girls who had slighted her in the past now invited her to lunch with them. They asked her to parties and treated her as though she were a person instead of a nothing. And when she was spoken to she found herself able to respond adequately.

What had happened? An enormous thing: metamorphosis. Her personality had been transformed. Fulfilled as a contributing member of society and no longer obsessed with her own shortcomings, she began to radiate respect for herself; and whoever has self-respect has respect. Gladys may remain a spinster but never again will she be a lonely, unhappy spinster. Her biggest job now is enrolling readers and she is very successful at it, for she feels the need deeply and nothing will stop her. Gladys has given herself away.

And now, briefly, one more story. John Smith (let us call him that) was a counter salesman in a leather goods shop. He was bright, he was doing a good job, he was learning the business so that one day he could open his own shop, he was happy. He was in the process of giving himself to himself, as our friend Mr. Conover had once been.

Then a bombshell burst. The city, through the power of eminent domain, ruled that all of the buildings on the block in which the shop in which John Smith worked had to be razed to make way for a bus terminal. John's boss said that this would put him out of business. After twenty years at that spot he had not the ambition or drive to start over again in a new location. John could have gone out for another job, but he was filled with the injustice of what was happening. There were ten or twelve other merchants on the block who would be more or less in the same fix as his boss. What of the years of labor and dedication they had expended? Was it all to go down the drain because some heartless city officials had decided that this was the only place for a terminal? Not while John had a breath of life in him.

First he polled the businessmen on the block. They all agreed to join him in a battle to get the city's decision rescinded. Then he called them and their customers to a rally in the assembly hall of a local public school. To this rally were invited the leaders of the opposition political party. A resolution was passed condemning the eminent domain proceedings and a committee was formed to find a site for the terminal that would serve the city's purpose without putting people out of business. John was recognized as the leader of the struggle and the party put its organization at his disposal.

A bitter fight was waged. In the course of the struggle it was discovered that two members of the City Council owned a part of the condemned property and stood to profit handsomely by the proceedings, as did another who was, apart from his part-time civic office, a lawyer who represented these two. John was up to his neck in the fight. Nothing else mattered. His boss even gave him leave with pay so he could devote all of his energy to it.

The scandal broke into the newspapers and John Smith's views were quoted over and over again. The whole city rose up in arms and the officials, at a hasty midnight meeting, voted to rescind the condemnation order. John went back to work, rewarded with a handsome raise.

The opposition party saw its opportunity to "throw the rascals out." In the quest for candidates one of the first names that came up was that of John Smith. Being a novice, he was not ready for important office but he was certainly suited to serve as a part-time Councilman. He was nominated and elected. That was just the beginning. Today he is a state senator. Tomorrow, who knows? His name may be known to you.

There are countless judges, mayors, governors and legislators who advanced in the political arena through their devoted participation in causes such as this, as well as in philanthropies, church activities, struggles for minority rights and what have you. They live full and fulfilled lives because they gave themselves away.

Try it yourself. Is there something in which you believe? Fight for it. Is there an injustice that pains you? Work to right it. Does your heart ache for people who need help? Help them.

Give yourself away. Once you do, you will find that you have been given back to yourself in a form much superior to the one you gave—a form that is much more attractive to all who see it than the old one was. It is a form with a new and improved personality.

Chapter Eleven

YOUR NEIGHBORS ARE NICE PEOPLE

❦ There is an old folk tale about a philosopher who lived in a tent on the edge of a Certain Town. One morning, just after dawn, a wayfarer approached the philosopher's tent. "Welcome to Certain Town," said the philosopher. "Do you come to visit or to remain among us?"

"That depends," said the wayfarer. "I must first know what sort of people live in Certain Town."

"H'm," h'med the philosopher. "And what sort of people live in the town from which you have come?"

"Ah," ahed the wayfarer, "they were good people all, kind and generous, thoughtful and considerate, wise and noble."

The philosopher smiled. "Carry on, Wayfarer," he said. "You will find exactly the same sort of people in Certain Town."

Later that day, along about sundown, another wayfarer approached the philosopher's tent. The philosopher welcomed him as he had welcomed the other, and asked whether he had come merely to visit or to remain.

"That depends," said the second wayfarer. "I should like to know what sort of people live here before I decide." To the philosopher's question about the people who lived in the town from which the wayfarer had come, the latter said: "They were all mean people, cruel and vindictive, selfish and greedy."

The philosopher gazed at him sadly. "I fear," he said, "that you will find exactly the same sort of people in Certain Town."

I am often reminded of this tale when I hear people saying, "My neighbors are impossible people. One of these days I'll move to another section." Brother, your neighbors will be exactly the same wherever you go; they will be very much like you. Oh, you might come upon a bad *neighbor* now and again, but bad *neighbors?* Never.

As a class or category, neighbors can and should provide a sort of human relationship that you obtain from no other group in your life, whether the group be friends, relatives, business associates, schoolmates or casual acquaintances outside your immediate neighborhood. Following, with a few slight revisions, is a list of neighborly qualities that was once handed to me by one of my own neighbors:

1. Neighbors do not intrude unless you specifically let it be known that you want them to. (The oc-

casional busybody neighbor is the exception who proves the general rule.)

2. Neighbors are *always there*. No matter how alone you may be in terms of friends and relatives, you are never actually alone when you have neighbors. Most of them respond eagerly to requests for help. Do you need a doctor in a hurry? Have you run out of tea bags just at the wrong moment? Do you expect a delivery you won't be home to receive? Have you locked yourself out of your apartment? Have you come home to find your place burglarized? Are you unable to leave a sick child to go to the drugstore for medicine? In short, do you need *somebody* right now, this very minute? Try a neighbor—you'll be delighted with the service.

3. Neighbors have many interests in common with you. What is good for you as a neighbor is good for them: lower taxes, better services, improved schools, neighborhood cleanliness and appearance, attractive gardens, convenient transportation, good shopping, reasonable prices for repairs, prompt snow removal and scores of other things. You need never find yourself at a loss for something to talk about with a neighbor.

4. Neighbors can help you save money. In the suburbs it is possible and practical for neighbors to own jointly such major implements as power mowers, snow blowers, electric hedge trimmers, power saws and the like instead of investing individually the full cost of a number of them. In the towns, neigh-

bors can pool their food and staple purchases to take advantage of quantity prices, exchange baby-sitting favors, trade magazines, share master television aerials, etc.

5. Neighbors, and only neighbors, can, if you have children, provide constant playmates for them—a precious service indeed.

6. Neighbors give you a sense of continuity and of *belonging*. There is something comfortable, relaxing and reassuring about coming home to your own neighborhood and seeing familiar faces in the street and at the windows, even if there be no one to greet you in your own home. The very sound of their radios and their occasional scrapping and the weeping of their kids makes you feel a part of the living, breathing world.

Surely your neighbors constitute a marvelous reservoir of pleasant association if only you are prepared to see their manifold merits and forgive them their occasional sins.

But remember our folk tale. To have good neighbors you must *be* a good neighbor. Despite their many virtues, neighbors are only human: they tend to respond in kind to the treatment they receive. If you snub them they will soon ignore you. If you refuse to come to their aid in the sort of emergencies mentioned above they will be reluctant to respond when you need *them*.

You may have seen some bad neighbors in your lifetime. For them a neighborhood becomes a kind of hell. If once they let their dogs out without a leash, half a dozen telephone calls are made to the authorities, though the same telephoners may pet your dog in the same situation if you happen to be a good neighbor. When they go out or when they return home they see only stony, unfriendly faces. If they play their radios a bit too loudly they are deluged with complaints. Their children are forbidden to trespass on the property of others and often denied the friendship of other children. If you did not know the reason for all of this you might believe that they lived in a neighborhood of "mean people, cruel and vindictive, selfish and greedy," in the words of our second wayfarer.

How do you become a good neighbor? Partly, of course, by being as ready and willing as the next one to be nice and agreeable and helpful. But in this aspect of living, as in all aspects, the colors are not merely black and white but many shades of gray in between, as well. It is possible to be too nice, too agreeable and too helpful. It is possible to expect too much of these qualities from your neighbors. Somewhere between too much and not enough is the right degree of neighborliness and you arrive at that point by experience, by trial and error and by the employment of that wonderful attribute—common sense.

Friends can be discarded, acquaintances can be exchanged for others and relatives (except those in one's immediate family) can be ignored. Neighbors are *there*, and there they remain, in the middle of your life all the time, unless you are prepared to go through the burdensome

and expensive process of packing your things, finding a
new neighborhood in which to live, and moving out, lock,
stock and dishes. And, as we already know, the neighbors
in the new place will be just the same, since they are always a reflection of yourself. It is better, far better, to
learn to be a good neighbor and to reap the reward of
having good neighbors.

Never visit a neighbor who is not already a friend until
you have been invited to do so. Far up on the list of undesirable neighbors is the one who makes it a habit to
"drop in" at whim. Every resident of a neighborhood
treasures and has the fullest right to his privacy. Take that
away from him and all of the good aspects of neighborhood life lose their importance. The fact that he is nice
and agreeable and helpful is the result of his need to overcome the "prison" aspect of neighborhood life as well as
of his inherent decency. If his privacy is violated in the
same way as a warden walks in at will on a real prisoner
in a cell, what can he gain from the fact that his caller is
pleasant and helpful? The very best neighborhoods are
those in which all the neighbors are friendly in a neighborly way, and not neighborly in the manner of an intimate friend. Neighborliness stops at the doorsill; beyond
that it becomes nuisance.

Does this mean that you should refrain from knocking
at your neighbor's door to ask the woman of the house
to do some shopping for you because your child is ill and
you can't get away; or borrowing a cupful of sugar on a

Sunday when you have company and the food shops are closed? Not at all. Neighbors consider social visits without invitation to be intrusion; they do not consider an approach for some neighborly assistance objectionable.

And yet, even this sort of thing can become a nuisance if engaged in too frequently. Emergency situations should not be confused with habitual carelessness or neglect. The woman who borrows a cup of sugar or a few tea bags once or twice a year, or the man who, on rare occasions, asks a neighbor to receive an express package for him, is behaving in a manner quite acceptable in almost any neighborhood. On the other hand, the woman who never remembers to keep an adequate stock of staples on hand and is forever borrowing, or the man who repeatedly imposes on his neighbor to accept his packages, becomes a pest in the eyes of his neighbor.

In neighborhoods in which people own their homes they are usually proud of their homes and their grounds. They take care of them tenderly and they work tirelessly to keep them in tip-top condition. They do not enjoy having dogs fouling up their pathways or children destroying the lovingly tended grass of their lawns. Even against their own wills they develop unfriendly feelings toward those who inflict such violations of good behavior on them. If you live in a neighborhood of one-family homes, do unto the property of others as you would have them do unto yours. If you live in the city, curb your dog. If you are a good neighbor in this respect, neighbors will try to make your children happy whenever they have an opportunity; and if your dog gets lost, they will get up a posse to find it instead of saying, "Wonderful."

If you are listening to your radio or TV, don't blast the whole neighborhood. If you participate in a car pool, don't miss your day for driving except in real emergencies. Don't park in a neighbor's driveway and warn visitors not to do it. In short, be considerate.

All of these cautionary notes are, in a way, of a negative character. They are intended merely to help you establish an aura of acceptability in the eyes of your neighbors so that when you go on to the positive program of projecting a better-than-average personality image in your neighborhood you may have a better chance for success. (If all you seek is the opportunity to live and let live, the chance to get along in your neighborhood without unpleasantness, the balance of this chapter will probably be of little interest to you.)

A few years ago I had the good fortune to observe a campaign conducted by a young couple who wanted to get a great deal more satisfaction out of neighborhood living than mere tolerant acceptance. Hy and Rosita Blant had two little children and a modest home. Hy Blant was a salesman for a tobacco supplies jobber and he worked very hard every day visiting tobacco shop after tobacco shop, taking orders and inducing the retailers to try new lines of merchandise.

Hy and his wife decided that until the children were old enough to go to high school the neighborhood in which they lived would be the heart of their social life. The physical demands of Hy's job, as well as the tiring labors of Rosita's as the mother of two active children and the chief cook and bottle washer of her home, were reason enough, they thought, to make it desirable that their social life did not make additional physical demands on their stamina. "Why should I travel ten or twenty or thirty miles to visit friends, and have to start earlier and get home later, when I can have my friends right at my door?" said Hy. "Why should I travel ten, twenty or thirty miles for cultural activity and amusement when I can have it right at my door?" said Rosita.

Hy and Rosita not only developed their own personalities in the process—they practically revolutionized the personality of the whole neighborhood.

They did nothing the first two months after they moved into the neighborhood but give the neighbors a chance to get used to their faces and their good behavior. Their place was well kept, their children were restrained from bothering other people, they had smiles for everyone they passed and soon everyone had smiles for them. They intruded on no one.

After two months they joined the local civic association and the P.T.A. This gave them an opportunity to be formally introduced to the people of the neighborhood and to engage in conversation with them at appropriate times. Each time Hy or Rosita found a kindred soul with whom communication was easy, pleasant and rewarding, the name went down in a little green notebook. Three names went into the book automatically: those of the neighbor to the right, the one to the left, and the one directly across the street.

When they had twelve names, they closed the book. Six months after their advent, they invited the twelve and their spouses to a buffet dinner party at their home. It was an expensive evening for Hy and Rosita but they considered the expense to be an investment in living. They had to hire two women to help and the food bill was rather a shocker but, as Hy said, "I'll save more than that in a year on train fares and gasoline."

It was an expensive evening but it was a fabulously successful evening. As Rosita explained it, "The fact that a name went into the notebook meant that the person was just our type. If they were all our type, they were naturally all one another's type. Everyone there knew everyone else but only casually, as a neighbor. This was the first time that they had all been together in one select group, without others whose tastes might differ, for a whole evening of relaxed socializing. You never saw such perfect mixing and rapport in your life. They didn't know exactly what it was that made it such a wonderful party, but what they did know was that it was our party, and that set us way up in their eyes. With this group we were made."

One of the guests was so happy about the whole thing that she convinced her husband it would be a good idea for them to run the same sort of party with the same congenial group. The party was given about a month later and it was just as successful. At the second party one of the guests remarked that since there were twelve couples and since they got along so well together, each couple might give one party a year for the group. Thus they could all be sure of one evening a month that could be guaranteed enjoyable, while the fuss and bother would come to each couple only once a year.

The idea was pounced upon by the others and the ball started to roll. No one dreamed then how far it would roll.

At the third party it was discovered that four of the men and two of the women could play musical instruments other than the piano, and that five all told could play the piano. Immediately plans were laid for a small orchestra that would practice once a week; the pianist was chosen by lot. Thus seven of the group were swept into a new and unexpected activity that they loved with all their hearts. They soon became quite proficient together and began to call themselves the Woodfield Neighborhood Orchestra. Word got around and the civic association induced the group to play at its annual get-together. Other neighbors, who were not a part of the original group of twelve couples, applied for membership in the orchestra and soon more than twenty who were sufficiently talented were accepted. Today the Woodfield Amateur Symphony is known and heard throughout the county and Hy and Rosita are known as its founders, though neither plays an instrument. "If it weren't for Hy and Rosita," said the first violinist, "we would never have got together in the first place."

An outgrowth of the orchestra was a dramatic club.

Perhaps out of some faint jealousy, one of the group who was not musical announced at one of the monthly parties that she had always wanted to be an actress. She said, "Why can't the rest of us work on a play? It's lots of fun, even if it turns out hammy." A dozen enthusiastic volunteers went to work on an old Broadway comedy. They enjoyed it so much that they talked about it wherever they went. One, who was a member of the local Rotary, offered to bring the company to the chapter's December dance. The play was a hit, though it is likely that a professional critic might have had doubts. There is now a permanent Woodfield Theatre Guild with its own playhouse, a converted loft in the business center of town. Credit? To Hy and Rosita, of course; and both are valued members of the cast. The Guild sometimes produces home-written plays by two of the original twenty-four guests at the Blant home who happen to have a talent for writing.

But Hy and Rosita have done much more in their neighborhood. Rosita established a baby-sitter's clearance club which now has a hundred subscribers. Each subscriber is honor-bound to baby-sit for other subscribers twice a month. Requests must be in the hands of the secretary a week in advance to give her sufficient time to locate a sitter who is free. This means that almost all the time any subscriber can have a baby-sitter twice a month, free, for there is no charge for membership and no charge for sitting. The secretaryship is rotated semimonthly so that no one has that irksome job more than once in about five years.

Hy established (first within the original group of twelve couples and later with the admission of dozens of others) an art exchange. Woodfield is probably the only neighborhood in which neighbors lend their cherished paintings back and forth for several weeks at a time. Those who are involved in the exchange derive a tremendous amount of pleasure and satisfaction from the opportunity to live periodically with different paintings in their homes.

As time goes by, people will forget who started all the excitement in Woodfield—they will just take it for granted that Woodfield happens to be a bit unusual. But that will not matter to Hy and Rosita, for they are so well established in the community by now and have such a secure place in the hearts of their neighbors that even they take such things for granted. Their case is an extreme one (actually I have altered one or two of their innovations because they were too wild to be generally useful) but it does serve as an illustration of the magnificent potential in neighborhood living for anyone who wishes to take advantage of it.

It was, of course, easier for Hy and Rosita together to capture an entire neighborhood than it would have been for a single individual. Married couples and neighborhoods have a natural affinity. But even those who are single or who are the adult children of married couples or who for any other reason are one instead of two can offer to and receive from neighbors additional blessings beyond the friendliness, the helpfulness and the familiarity that are the normal fruits of neighborliness.

A survey among single folk indicates that next to good health the blessings they want more than anything else are: a husband or a wife, a good job and a good time. Good neighbors are often fountains from which these blessings flow.

Jane Austen, in *Pride and Prejudice,* wrote: "It is a truth, universally acknowledged, that a single man in possession of a good fortune [she might have substituted broad shoulders or a handsome face, or a pleasing personality, and she might have spoken of a single woman as well] must be in want of a wife. However little known the feelings or views of such a man may be on his first entering a neighborhood, this truth is so well fixed in the minds of the surrounding families that he is considered as the rightful property of some one or other of their daughters."

It is quite true that if you are a good neighbor your fellow neighbors have a sort of pride of possession in you. If you are genuinely one of them they simply cannot bear to see you remain unattached, and it becomes for them a solemn duty to find a husband or a wife for you; and since there are so many of them, bless them, their chances of success are somewhat better than average.

By the same token, they are eager to see you cheerful and happy until such time as you are espoused. You are bound to have good times if you are unbending enough to participate in the activities for younger folk on which the older neighborhood folk expend so much of their time, their money, their energy and their dedication.

As for jobs, practically every neighbor has an association with a profession or business concern; in many cases they are employers themselves. If you have found your niche in the neighborhood, they are likely to know more about you (and be pleased with what they know) than they do about job-seekers who come to their knowledge from the less warm world outside the neighborhood. In my own experience, almost everyone I know has at one time or another in his life obtained a position through the good offices of a neighbor.

What do they want from you in return? Very little beyond good cheer, a measure of respect, and the courtesies of a normal neighbor. If sometimes you lend a hand with a baby carriage, or help one of their children with his homework, or sit with a child of an evening, they will positively dote on you.

Rich or poor, single or married, young, middle-aged or elderly, you have and you will have neighbors. Take them to your heart and they will take you to their hearts. Cast them aside and you become yourself an outcast.

The Bible itself tells you: Love thy neighbor as thyself.

Chapter Twelve

MUST YOU LEAVE? HERE'S YOUR HAT

❧ I have always been puzzled by a contradiction in American life. We are by nature a gregarious people—perhaps the most gregarious in the world. We are known for visiting back and forth on a colossal scale; for calling one another by our given names on the briefest acquaintanceship; for joining clubs and schools and associations and causes at the drop of a hat; for congregating at rallies and meetings and concerts and theatres and athletic fields in huge numbers. And yet in spite of all this frantic togetherness we have more lonely people per square mile than you can count.

The only thing that can account for this contradiction, it seems to me, is the fact that we are just as much apart when we are together as we are when we are alone. Our human contact is superficial and unsatisfying. We meet on the surface rather than in depth. We take the shadow and miss the substance of companionship. In brief, we don't seem to understand what this togetherness we are always talking about really means. The search for companionship reaches the zenith of absurdity when we gather together in a darkish room before a television screen, thus eliminating even the slight bond of empty conversation.

In this chapter we shall attempt to remedy the situation at least in your home and in the homes of the people you visit. We shall take steps to make you the sort of host or hostess whose guests (and you, yourself) are not merely going through the motions of visiting together as a sort of meaningless ritual but are so thoroughly savoring the companionship that all of you will want to repeat the experience again and again; and to make you the sort of guest who will be so satisfying to your hosts that whenever they get up a guest list your name will be the first to pop into their heads.

Washington Irving described true hospitality as the "breaking through the chills of ceremony and selfishness, and thawing every heart into a flow." There is an emanation from the heart, he said, "that cannot be described, but is immediately felt, and puts the stranger at once at his ease." And Clarendon explained that "it is not the quantity of the meat but the cheerfulness of the guests which makes the feast." These pearls of wisdom are precious, and they should be kept always in mind when you have guests at your home; the trick, however, is to know *how* to thaw every heart and make the guests cheerful. You cannot accomplish it merely by willing it or by the goodness of your heart. You have to go about it with a measure of technique, as well.

Your life as a host (we shall use the word for both men and women, though perhaps it would be more suitable to use the word "hostess" since more entertaining at home is done by women than by men) will encompass two major phases:

1. Being host to one or two guests.
2. Being host to more than two guests.

We can dispose of the first phase with comparative dispatch. When one or two people come to visit you the demands upon your attention are so narrow that there is practically no problem. It is easy to make guests happy when they can have you completely to themselves. All you have to do is feed them, talk to them, listen to them, laugh at their jokes and cluck your tongue at their sorrows. No visitor can expect or hope for or even want more when the party is so small. Formal plans of any sort would be absurd.

So—you can hardly fail to be a successful host to one or two visitors. On the other hand, anybody can be a good host to one or a couple, so unless you have an exceptionally scintillating personality you will never gain a reputation as a host by limiting yourself to one or two guests at a time. This is not to say that you should always attempt to entertain on a larger scale. Having one or two dear friends over for an evening can be one of the most satisfying experiences for all concerned. However, we must always keep in mind that our purpose in this volume is limited to action that will help to develop your personality and solve problems of loneliness. There are no such problems connected with dear and intimate friends. We are concerned here with the effort to bring more intimately into your life people who are not already close to you; and this can be accomplished more readily, in terms of hospitality, by entertaining on a slightly larger scale.

How large a scale? That depends. It depends on how much room you have, how much you can afford to spend, how much help you can get, and how much energy you have. In addition, it depends on what you are trying to accomplish. If you are merely interested in paying off a number of social obligations and if you have a large home and lots of money and if you don't care whether your guests enjoy themselves or not, you can entertain a hundred people at one time, wipe the slate clean, and go to bed satisfied with yourself. Perhaps a number of your guests might have a very good time, but even if they did it would be only vaguely related in their minds with *you*.

For a pleasant evening, which all will savor and delight in, a group of eight is perhaps the ideal. That doesn't rule out six or ten or twelve; there cannot be absolutes in matters like this. I propose eight as the ideal number as

206 DEVELOPING YOUR PERSONALITY

the result of an informal survey among a score of women who entertain frequently and who have some very definite ideas on the art of "hosting." I doubt whether any of them entertains as a technique for overcoming loneliness, but all of them manage to achieve the end result for which we are working. Some of the women preferred six, others ten or twelve. It averaged out at eight, and following are some of the reasons given. A few of them are especially relevant to our purpose:

1. It doesn't wear me out when I entertain a group of that size. My kitchen facilities are not taxed; I have room at the table and I don't have to worry about whether or not I have enough service. When I entertain a large group, I'm completely pooped, and I can't enjoy myself and nobody enjoys me. I do ten times as much work and I spend most of my time apologizing for things that aren't right. When it's all over I feel miserable because I'm sure it has been a flop.

2. With eight people you have one group. It doesn't have to split up into cliques. At larger parties, people have to clique up and a lot of people always have the notion that the people in another clique are having a better time, so the party is spoiled for them. I find that eight people are the most who can become involved in a single discussion or friendly argument. With only that many people, there is time for everyone to have his say and it is easy for everyone to hear what the others are saying. When the evening is finished everyone has the feeling that not only has he had a good time but he has also con-

tributed something to the enjoyment of the others. Also, they get the feeling that there has been some mental stimulation instead of just eating and drinking and "having fun." They call me the next day and tell me how wonderful I am and I know they mean it.

3. If you like to have some organized amusement at a party, like games or cards, you can do it best with eight people. With a larger group it becomes unruly, and with less people it just doesn't seem to be as much fun. Personally, I don't like cards at my parties, but if you happen to have people over who do like cards, two tables is just right. One table makes it a card game instead of a party and more than two tables makes me feel like I'm running a gambling casino. In any event, I never arrange things so that my guests spend more than half the evening at cards. The same is true of games. A whole evening of games is like running a playground. A few intelligent games are fun. Every party has to be at least half general conversation. People don't seem to realize any more how much fun it is just to talk.

4. I like to limit my parties to eight people for a lot of little reasons that may seem silly to some people, but I have found that often it is the little things that make the difference between perfection and just all right. For instance, ice cubes. You have no idea how fast they go with a large crowd. I know that some people can run out to the corner and buy more, or that others have fancy, expensive ice-cube gadgets, but I can't and I don't. And somehow I never seem to have enough ashtrays around for a large

group. Of course I could buy a few dozen, but why should I clutter up my house with ashtrays merely because I might need them once a year or less? It's better to invite less people. And by the way, ashtrays fill up and have to be emptied out. I once spent practically the whole evening emptying ashtrays while all my guests were feeling too sorry for me to enjoy themselves.

5. Large parties are too expensive. It's not what you think. I mean that it costs four times as much to entertain sixteen people as it does to entertain eight. Why? I'll tell you. In the first place, liquor. You may not believe it, but people who are t.. wallflower type, who are left out, sort of, drink far more than those who are participating, both because they need it to keep up their spirits and because it gives them the appearance of not being left out—you know, that they like to drink and that they are doing what they like to do. Liquor is the most expensive item at any party. And at big parties there are always some guests who do nothing but drink all evening. Then, again, I can't handle a large group without help, so I have to pay for a maid. As for food, I like everyone to have enough, but when there are many people there is a disproportionate amount of waste. I have to buy and prepare much more than you would think. And I never had a large party yet at which there wasn't damage from stains and cigarette burns and breakage. People in large groups are more careless. And that's an additional expense.

Obviously I have not reported all this in such great detail merely to demonstrate that there is something magical about the figure eight. In the comments of the women to whom I spoke there are a number of bits of incidental intelligence that can be most valuable to you in your effort to entertain in such a manner as to bring your guests so close to you that you become an important part of their lives. Let us extract and examine a few of them.

1. *You should be as fresh and alert as possible when you are the host.*

From the point of view of your own interests, entertaining is a waste of your time if you are merely the drudge who does all the work and has no pep left to shine when the guests arrive. The host must be the star of the party. Note that I did not say the life of the party. It is your job to see to it that everyone has a good time and you can do that job only if you are not too tired. If there is a lapse in the conversation or activity, you should be ready and able to step into the breach. Everyone should be aware of your presence, though others may be permitted (and should be permitted) to take the center of the stage. Indeed, you should subtly direct each one to the center of the stage at one time or another.

For instance, when a silence falls, you could say something like this: "By the way, I meant to tell all of you about Dot. She's going to college in Geneva and she asked me if I could tell her about what clothes to take along. I think your sister went to school in Switzerland, Sue. How did she dress?"

That gives Sue the center of the stage and brings her

a bit closer to you. Please—before you attack, let me say I know that it is most unlikely that you are going to be able to find such fortunate opportunities as this one very often during the course of an evening. But with a little ingenuity you can achieve the same effect many times. You might refer to an item of food you have served and ask one of the guests whether she made it the same way. Or you could comment on the aroma of a guest's cigar in this way: "That must be a very good cigar. Most of the time I don't like cigars. Is yours something special?" (When you lead a cigar smoker into the subject of cigars you have usually made him a happy man.) If you are wide-awake and fresh, you can keep the party from ever bogging down into an awkward silence.

Moreover, you can save your guests from uncomfortable moments that might otherwise leave them with vaguely unpleasant memories of your party. One may have a long ash with no tray nearby, another may be lacking a napkin, another may be sitting with an empty glass —too shy to ask for a refill, etc. If you aren't worn out before the party starts you will notice all these things and take care of them in time.

You may ask how one prepares a party for eight and remains fresh and untired. There is no scientific method. Entertaining is always hard and tiring work. I would say that foresight and pacing are the indispensable ingredients. Always do your inviting well in advance of your party. Then you can make your preparations at your convenience as you go along. It is the necessity for doing everything all at once and in a hurry that makes for the most nervousness and weariness.

Write down a list of the things you have to buy and do. Buy them and do them unhurriedly, checking off the items you have completed. The knowledge that you have left nothing undone and will not be subjected to unexpected embarrassment will of itself help to keep you fresh.

If you plan to serve a meal, there are some things like special desserts and appetizers and hors d'oeuvres that can be prepared well in advance and kept fresh with waxed paper and refrigeration.

In short, see to it that entertaining is as much of a joy as it is a chore. If it is a joy for you, it will be a joy for all.

2. *The best parties are those at which all the guests can be participating members of a single, homogeneous group.*

Limiting the number of guests to eight will not be enough to accomplish this, though a larger number will make it more difficult and a really large number impossible. It is your responsibility, as host, to bring together people who will mix, who have similar interests, tastes and levels of intelligence and education. Apart from the fact that such people are far more likely to have a good time together than a radically mixed group, it is unkind to have guests with lesser capabilities or disparate interests struggling through an evening with the others, feeling inadequate and resentful. Surely you should not limit your friendships on the basis of snobbishness, but it isn't necessary for you to go to the extent of attempting the impossible task of mixing oil with water.

Try to have one major theme for every gathering. It should be one that will appeal to all your guests but it should be planned to consume only a portion of the evening, leaving the rest of the time for spontaneous discussion and activity. Such a theme can assume a wide variety of forms, each a potent factor toward taking advantage of and strengthening the homogeneity of your group. Following are a few of the themes utilized at one time or another by the women I mentioned.

A. I'm a pretty good cook, if I do say it myself. Often when I invite people over, I tell them it is to be a French evening or an Italian evening or a Spanish evening, or something like that. Then, out of an international cookbook that I have, I select and prepare meals of the particular nationality involved. You have no idea what a stimulus this is to conversation. If some of my guests have traveled, they usually take the meal as a cue to tell us some interesting things about the countries they have visited. Others ask questions and the talk sparkles. Very often I am asked for the recipes and I give them freely without saying I got them out of a book. If that's a lie, it's a very small and very white lie. You've no idea what a reputation I have as a cook! People talk about my dinners long afterward and I confess I enjoy the feeling.

Sometimes I try to have extra little international touches. For instance, though I think the use of paper napkins at a party is not right as a rule, I don't mind using those clever ones with foreign sayings on them on my international evenings. I may get a few French or Italian or Spanish recordings and play them during or after the meal. If one of my friends has visited the particular country, I get her to bring her pictures, with a fifteen-minute time limit. I have found that no one wants to look at other people's pictures longer than that.

B. Whenever I become friendly with someone who has had an especially interesting experience, or who has some special knowledge or talent, I make it a point to invite him or her over when I am having a group that I think would be interested. I don't mean professional entertainers or musicians, for in their case it would be an imposition. I mean ordinary people who are pleased and flattered when you ask them to be the center of attention at a party. Then, when I invite my friends I tell them about this special treat and it goes over very well. For example, I once had as guests a young couple who had been to Tokyo. The stories they told us about geishas and pearls and the strange customs, as well as the trend toward westernization, so stimulated the other guests that though I tried to change the subject they wouldn't leave it. It was just like having a travel lecturer, but without the stiffness and formality of a lecture. Everyone not only had a good time but felt that it was an evening well and profitably spent from the intellectual standpoint.

C. As you can see, I'm not as young as I used to be, and most of my friends are of my age, approximately. I have noticed an interesting thing about people who get on toward middle age—they become nostalgic. They like to remember the things they did and the things that happened in the days of their youth. Well, when I entertain, I sometimes cater to that nostalgia, without saying so directly, of course. I have a large collection of sheet music, songs published and popular when we were young. It might amaze you to know that my friends and I remember the lyrics of literally hundreds of the old songs, though we couldn't sing a rock and roll number to save our lives.

Well, I invite my friends over for dinner and then I take out the old songs and hit the keys. You've no idea how much they enjoy singing along for an hour or so. One of them now calls these evenings "Sing Along with Madge" evenings. There were a few who didn't care too much for this sort of amusement. I invite them at other times now. Those who do like it can't wait for the next invitation.

3. *Every party has to be at least half general conversation.*

As I have indicated more than once, Americans are a paradoxical people. Here's another illustration. The average American enjoys almost more than anything else the opportunity to engage in fairly intelligent conversation. I refer to fairly intelligent Americans, of course, and I believe most Americans are at least fairly intelligent despite the herculean efforts they make to hide it. It is not conceivable that a people that was less than intelligent could have built up the greatest country in the world. And yet, loving good conversation as they do, they enjoy less of it than almost any other people in the world. Oh, they do manage to get in an inordinate amount of small talk when they get a moment away from television or radio or theatre or cards or sports or work; but that isn't conversation —it's just talk.

However, get a group of them into a corner with nothing else to distract them (I guess the trouble really is that half the people of the country are engaged in the business of distracting the other half with the interests and diversions they have to sell), and lead them into a real conversation, and they will respond with such vigor and intelligence and enjoyment that you will be amazed. It is not easy to get them started; they have to be forced at first because they are so long out of practice. But once they recapture the knack they go all out.

Later in this chapter we shall take up the art of conversation as it applies to you. At this point it is important only to note that Americans do love good conversation and if you are the one who is responsible for seeing to it that they get it, they will love you for it. I do believe that of all hosts, the most successful by far are those who stimulate conversation when they entertain.

You can fall down on every other phase of entertainment, even those which I have outlined above, and still be one of the best of all hosts if there is good talk at your parties. Whatever else you do or fail to do, leave plenty of room and offer plenty of opportunity and stimulation for the exchange of ideas and opinions.

4. A few intelligent games are fun.

Most people think that games are just for kids; and so they are—if they are kid games. But it would not be at all silly to involve your guests in a game or two designed for adults. Some ingenious hosts I know manage to invent such games. Others buy, borrow or copy them.

A game suitable for adults must have one or more features like these: a challenge to the intelligence; an opportunity to learn something useful; some hints on self-improvement; the aura of entertainment; and, practically invariably, the element of competition. A game that has no result, that peters out into nothingness, leaves the players feeling flat and disappointed. There should be winners or, at the least, some who have demonstrated superiority in the playing. The main thing to avoid in a game is one that is frequently not avoided even by intelligent players: hurting the sensibilities of one or more of the players. A game that brings any sort of pain to a participant is not really a game; it is a perversion of all that a game is supposed to be.

There are many books and other sources from which you can select numerous games that will meet the requirements referred to above, and so there would be little point in attempting to set any considerable number down on these pages. Perhaps two illustrations, one of the wrong kind of game and one of the right kind, will serve to set you on the track.

I once attended a party at which the host announced that we were to play a game called Revelation. We were all to write down on a sheet of paper revealing facts about our respective spouses and sign our names. The papers were handed in to the host, who was to read them aloud without telling the names signed to the revelations. The husbands and wives were then to guess which of the revelations had been written about themselves. This would show how accurately they understood what their spouses thought of them.

The game was moderately enjoyable as it went along, though several times we were on rather thin ice. Then the host read this one out: "My wife thinks she is beautiful." A pretty woman who was present smiled and called out, "My husband must have written that."

"Wrong," said the host. We all began to get a bit nervous. "Anybody else want to guess?"

There was silence. No one wanted to claim the author of the revelation as her husband. There were two exceedingly plain women among us and unconsciously some of the others looked their way. The two plain women blushed in embarrassed self-consciousness. The rules of the game forbade the host to reveal the name of the writer unless he had been correctly claimed by his wife. A cold damper seemed to fall upon the party and pretty soon we began to make excuses for having to leave early. We were all uncomfortable, including our host.

This game lacked almost all of the positive elements that a parlor game should have and contained the one negative element that no parlor game should ever have: the capacity to bring hurt or shame or pain to a player.

There was no real competition; we couldn't learn anything worth learning from the game; there was little challenge to the intelligence; there was no opportunity for self-improvement. There was a moderate entertainment value that was too risky to be enjoyed.

On the other hand, there was another gathering not long after at which I participated in a game which was amusing, mentally challenging, competitive and somewhat instructive. It was a simple game but it gave us all a great deal of pleasure without any danger at all that a guest could be hurt.

We were all seated about a table with pencil and paper and asked to write down a colloquialism or a slang expression. Each of us was then to pass our sheet to the person at our left who, in turn, was to rewrite the expression into "highbrow" English. Then, one at a time, we were to read our translation aloud and the first one to guess what the original colloquialism was would be given ten points. Of course, in each case the person who had written the original expression, that is, the person at the right of the reader and translator, was barred from guessing. The one with the highest number of points at the end would be the winner.

Here is how it went. I wrote *I get it* and the translator to my left rewrote it as follows: *That which you have just imparted to me has struck a chord of comprehension within my cerebellum.*

Another guest wrote *Easy come, easy go*, which was transformed into: *Rewards which come to one who has made little effort or sacrifice to win them are ordinarily lost with as little difficulty.*

As I say, there are literally thousands of good party games and many books in which to find them. Try a good one now and then. It will pay off or as one might translate it, "You will find it yielding of a gratifying profit."

5. *Don't be too busy doing little things like filling glasses and emptying ashtrays to be a part of your own party.*

Plan your evening so you will have plenty of time to sit with your guests and sparkle as brightly as any of them. Naturally, there will be some things which, as host, you will simply have to do while the others are busy having fun. That is the penalty of being a host. The true art of participating in your own parties is, however, the ability to cut down to the barest minimum your intervals as worker instead of enjoyer. Here are a few hints that should be helpful:

A. Gentlemen guests love to be considered talented bartenders. Just say cheerily, "Johnny, you're in charge of the bar tonight." Then announce to the others, "Anyone wants a drink, he asks Johnny. Johnny's bartender tonight." If Johnny doesn't want to do it he will probably protest that he's the worst bartender in town, but most of the time Johnny will love it. Don't be afraid to do this—it will help to break the ice all around.

B. Use a tea wagon to cart stuff like late-evening coffee or fruit or snacks from kitchen to living room. This is much better than running back and forth endlessly with cups and saucers and utensils, etc.

c. If you have to do your own dishes, do them after the party is over. Never retire to the kitchen for a dish-washing spree while the party is on. In the first place, you'll be out of the party, and in the second place, you will have all your guests feeling sorry for you and guilty. If there is anything you don't want, it is pity.

With these as a starter, you will undoubtedly figure out additional ways of sparing yourself the tiny chores that add up to so much time away from the festivities.

Just as there are books on games, so there are many books on the art of being a host. If you are interested in the art of entertaining for its own sake, go to these books. What I have tried to do in these pages, and all I have tried to do, is to extract from the whole broad field of home entertaining only those elements which will, while they help you to be a better host, help you to establish the sort of rapport with your guests that will make them fond of you and desirous of your company. With such people in your life, you need never be lonely again.

Fortunately, every host is just as often a guest, free of the responsibilities that beset the host. That is only fair, and now we are going to make you just as good a guest as you are a host. Actually, it is harder to be a good guest, but it is easier to tell you how. The reason is that most of the pointers on entertaining are of a technical nature, and while they are numerous in the telling they are not too difficult to grasp and put into effect. There are only a few things to tell you about being a good guest, but most of them require personality development and readjustment, a difficult assignment at best. We shall not go into the obvious clichés about arriving punctually, departing at a reasonable hour and the like. Any work on etiquette will fill you in on such matters, if you need such help— and I doubt that you do.

1. When you arrive, appear pleased that you have been invited. But don't gush and don't sound overly grateful. Don't rave wildly about the beauty of the home and don't flatter unduly. Take your presence as a matter of course, as though people visit one another all the time. They do, you know. Your host will think more of you for your self-assurance, and any pleasant comment you *do* make will be taken more seriously and appreciated more deeply.

In the suburb in which I live there is a woman who just bowls you over with her exuberant appreciation every time you invite her to your home. To listen to her is to squirm: "Oh, how wonderful to see you. I'm so glad you asked me to come. I'm sure it will be a wonderful party. You look simply wonderful"—and on and on. We all know everything can't be *that* wonderful, so we don't take *anything* she says very seriously. We invite her when we have to, which is too often, because we are kindhearted. But you wouldn't want anyone inviting *you* over out of mere kindness.

2. On the other hand, don't be critical unless you are asked for your opinion; even then, if your opinion is un-

favorable, tell a little white lie. If you don't care for the food, don't say anything unless you are asked. If you are asked, simply say you think it is quite good. If your host asks your opinion of a bratty child, just smile benignly. If you haven't seen the home before, and if you don't think it is any great shakes, and if you are asked to say what you think, say you like it very much.

It's a wonderful thing that everyone thinks his own food, his own home, his own kids, his own pets, his own car and his own neighborhood are the very best. You'll never change his mind by disagreeing; you'll only get him to think you are either not very nice or not very bright. Don't gush, but don't crush.

3. It is always in order to bring a little gift. It doesn't have to be expensive and it doesn't have to be unusual. If there are children, the gift should be for them, whether it be chocolates, toys or books. Never mind the older folk. You probably won't find this advice in any book of etiquette, but take my word for it, there is nothing more pleasing to a host than some special attention to his children, who are always the most wonderful children of all.

If there are no children, it is appropriate to bring any conventional gift, like a box of chocolates, a book, or some flowers. You are not out to establish a reputation for originality in the art of giving gifts. All you are trying to do is to make a gracious little unobtrusive gesture that pleases your host for no reason other than that you were thoughtful enough to bring *something*. It is a series of small but pleasant and comfortable acts that gradually, subtly and unconsciously win you a special place in the hearts of others, particularly in the hearts of hosts, who are so eager for you to be pleased that nothing pleases them more than little actions that seem to please you in the doing.

4. Learn to converse intelligently and enjoyably. The host can always shift the burden of conversation on to his guests; and the guests must be equipped to accept the burden.

If you are not naturally a glib or facile talker, this may be difficult. Of one thing you can be certain, however, and that is that it will be easier for you to engage in conversation if you have something to say. You may not become silver-tongued but at least your tongue won't have to stay locked up for the evening.

Next to children, clothes, pets, and the weather, perhaps the most frequent topic of conversation is the news. (As your circle of friends expands and as you begin to travel in more knowledgeable society, it will be necessary for you to learn to engage in more than such small talk. We shall pursue this aspect of your personality development more thoroughly in Chapter Fifteen.) Read a good paper every day, even if you can manage to read only the front page and the editorial page. You do not have to be conversant with everything that happens, but you will be marked less than adequate if you cannot participate in conversations on matters important enough to be published on page one of your newspaper. The editorial columns will give you analyses and commentary that you can quote in agreement or disagreement with the remarks of others; and you can do this with or without giving credit to the paper. The good conversationalist is one who not only knows what is happening but also has some definite opinions about it.

In expressing your opinions, don't be opinionated. It does no harm to preface your opinions with "I think" or "It seems to me," but it can do you a great deal of harm socially to pontificate or hand your opinions down as gospel from on high.

After the news, people in informed circles speak most frequently of books. The person who cannot join in a discussion of the leading books of the day—or the classics of old, for that matter—will have to be silent and uncomfortable much of the time. (In Chapter Fifteen you will find a formula that, hopefully, will make it possible for you to hold your own in any ordinary conversation about books and, for that matter, music, art and other topics that lend spice as well as substance to social intercourse.)

It is important to understand that while small talk becomes tiresome and even boring when engaged in to the exclusion of more erudite conversation, it should not be disdained altogether. If you went to a party and talked only about books and the drama and the arts and other learned subjects, people might come to consider you a bit queer. Trivial chatter, harmless gossip and kidding around are just as much enjoyed (in moderation) as intellectual talk even in groups with the highest brows. Your goal should be to become a contributing member of any average group engaged in a period of average discussion on the average topics that such a group normally discusses; and, on occasion, a respected participant in discussions that rise a bit above the average. As such a person, you will be a most-wanted and most-favored guest.

5. Ask for favors. Yes, that is exactly what you have just read: ask for favors. I have said more than once in these pages that the thing that pleases people most is the knowledge that they are pleasing others.

What sort of favors? Little ones. Favors that will not be too much of a bother. Favors that will make your host feel like a benefactor without too much effort: "I've brought my new skirt along and I have to shorten it. It's pinned up at the hem but I don't think it's quite straight all around. Could I impose on you to shift a few of the pins so it will be straight when I sew it?"

Or: "Could I have just a pipeful of the tobacco you are smoking? I'd like to get some myself. Where do you buy it?"

Or: "I've got to go to Boston. I know you drive up often. Would you be good enough to write out the route for me?"

Most people know subconsciously, if they are not aware of it consciously, that the people least willing to accept favors are the people least willing to give them. The converse is also true. We always feel, when people ask us to do little things for them, that they would do little things for us quite as a matter of course.

It is not intended here to advise you to think up little favors merely as a gimmick to make people like you. What is intended is the advice that if there *are* any small favors you would like from your host, don't hesitate to ask.

6. Participate. You remember our wet-blanket questionnaire? If your host decides on a game, or an activity, or a discussion, join in. Make it easier for him. He has a tough job on his hands. Don't be a holdout. If it is shyness that is holding you back from participation, pretend you are about to commit suicide and plunge. You'll be so relieved to come out of it alive that the next time will be easier. If it is lack of skill that holds you back, remember that often the most fun in any activity comes from the antics of the unskilled; and that you'll never achieve skill without the initial awkward practice. That goes for singing, reciting, solving puzzles, talking or whatever other torture your host chooses to inflict.

7. Go home when you have said good-bye. The good impression of a whole evening can be destroyed by a guest who says good-bye and stands talking and talking at the doorway, keeping the host either from the other guests or from bed. It is almost as bad to say good-bye and not leave as it is to leave without saying good-bye.

If you take seriously your obligations as a guest, you will find your friends saying, with the great poet Shelley, though not in exactly the same words:

> You must come home with me and be my guest;
> You will give joy to me, and I will do
> All that is in my power to honor you.

Chapter Thirteen

EIGHT HOURS A DAY

❧ About forty years ago, Kahlil Gibran, a Syrian-born poet, painter, philosopher and fighter for social justice who had settled in the United States, gave the world a message. "Work," he wrote, "is love made visible. And if you cannot work with love but only with distaste, it is better that you should leave your work and sit at the gate of the temple and take alms of those who work with joy."

"Sure," you may reply. "It's easy to tell other people to go out and beg if they don't love their work. But most of us have to make a living for ourselves and our families and few of us are fortunate enough to have work that we love."

Well, the first thing we must learn in this world if we are to get the most out of our lives is to be practical and sensible. In the matter of working for a living at a job you do not love, the answer is not, as Gibran seems to suggest, to quit your job and become a mendicant but rather—and it may be that this is what he really means when he says "if you cannot work with love"—to do your level best so to alter and adjust to your work environment as to be able to work with love, even though you do not love the work *per se*.

By now you have guessed the solution: it is in your relations with your colleagues. If you come into an office or a shop or even, as a laborer, into a trench you are digging, and are greeted warmly by co-workers who like you and whom you like, you have already succeeded in the establishment of an environment that takes much of the edge off your dislike of your work-world. Conversely, if your co-workers distrust you, or are jealous of you, or fear you, or merely are disinterested in you, there is no offset and the work becomes ever more distasteful. In fact, even if you are doing exactly the sort of work you like best it can become distasteful to you if your lines of communication with your colleagues are down.

What follows, therefore, applies equally to all people who work with others, whether they like their work or not. For eight hours a day, more or less, you live in the world of colleagues—do what you can to help them make it the best of all possible worlds.

To launch this project, try measuring yourself as a colleague *vis-à-vis* the others. You can start with a negative approach. There are certain common failings in the attitudes of workers that almost invariably contribute to unpopularity on the job. Do you have some of these failings? Do you have many of them? If you have to answer "Yes" to more than six of the following questions you must be having a rather difficult time getting along with the others. If you give more than twelve positive replies your plight is serious, and you will never be happy on a job unless your skin is an inch thick or unless you take radical steps toward reform.

1. If a woman, are you coy with the boss, and a bit flirtatious? If a man, do you kowtow visibly?

2. Do you eat more at lunch when the check is divided evenly among the diners than you do when there are separate checks?

3. Do you frequently ask colleagues to cover for you while you slip out on a personal errand?

4. Do you make it a habit to report minor infractions by others to your superior?

5. Do you ostentatiously carry a heavier work load than other conscientious workers?

6. When your own work eases up, do you make a habit of visiting others who are busy and engaging them in conversation?

7. Do you have extreme window habits? That is, do you insist on a wide-open window in zero weather or a tightly shut window in the dog days of summer?

8. Do you take advantage of every lull to tell jokes?

9. Are you secretive, morose, gloomy or unsociable?

10. Do you pepper your conversation with profanity?

11. Do you boast of your weekend escapades?

12. Are you careless about bathing?

13. Are you affected in your manner or speech?

14. Do you increase the work load of others through frequent absence?

15. Do you gossip to some of your colleagues about others?

16. Do you betray confidences?

17. Do you come to the office or shop when you have a runny, sneezy, coughy cold?

18. Do you often stay on when the others have left?

19. Do you pick up papers from the desks of others and read them?

20. Do you blame others for your mistakes?

21. Do you comment unfavorably on the clothing or appearance of others?

22. Do you dress for the office as though you were going to a ball? If female, do you overexpose your body?

23. Are you too easily insulted?

24. Do you boast of your relationship to one of the higher-ups?

25. Do you speak too loudly at the telephone?

Sometimes it is possible to overcome a few negative attributes through the possession of laudable traits. The more "Yes" answers you can give to the following questions, the more likely you are to love working even though you may not love your work.

1. Are you usually ready to alter your lunch hour to accommodate a colleague?

2. Do you remember the birthdays of your colleagues with at least greeting cards?

3. Are you willing to lend small sums "until payday"?

4. Do you occasionally help a colleague who is temporarily overloaded with work?

5. Are you a good listener?

6. Do you tell your associates about good books you have read or good shows you have seen?

7. Are you agreeable about contributing to office collections for colleagues?

8. In the shop, do you stop to lend a hand with a heavy object or a broken machine?

9. Do you participate in the group activities of the gang?

10. Do you refrain from prying?

11. Do you visit colleagues when they are ill?

12. Do you eschew heavy perfumes?

13. Are you cheerful?

14. Can you take a bit of ribbing?

15. Do you make suggestions that serve to ease the work of others?

16. Are you respectful of the dignity of those you outrank?

17. Are you modest?

18. Do you tell little white lies to spare the feelings of colleagues?

19. Do your co-workers feel they can depend on you?

20. Do you invite colleagues to your home occasionally and do you accept their invitations?

232 DEVELOPING YOUR PERSONALITY

21. When you are on vacation, do you send cards to the office or shop?

22. Are you enthusiastic?

23. Are you neat about your person and your work area?

24. Do you do a full day's work? (Colleagues resent those who goof off while they themselves give a day's work for a day's pay.)

25. Do you sometimes arrange a double date and include a colleague who may be having a bit of difficulty in that department?

It is clear from the above that the only difference between making your way in the world of colleagues and making it in your other worlds is that of detail, with the details in some instances overlapping. It all boils down to being friendly, helpful and decent and to being willing to accept friendliness, helpfulness and decency. Each world has its own technical peculiarities and it is your job to see and understand them.

One word of caution: it never pays to overdo. One must always remember that even friendliness and helpfulness can become a bore and a nuisance. The eager beaver is often as unpopular as the lone wolf. In many places of employment there is a worker who is known as the pest. Rarely does he know why he is avoided. Isn't he forever at someone's elbow offering advice, assistance, friendship and entertainment? Doesn't his heart flow over with love for his fellow workers? Does he ever leave them out of his innermost thoughts? Doesn't he always tell them everything and isn't he always interested in everything about them?

You see? The very listing of his superior qualities becomes his condemnation. People at work are people at *work*. The work has to get done, like it or not. They will welcome and be grateful for the presence of colleagues who are good and kind and considerate and friendly, but they cannot tolerate being overwhelmed by or drowned in these virtues.

Even your passive qualities can be oppressive. Are you neat and clean in your person and in your work area? If you are, fine. But if you are forever washing your hands and cleaning your nails and dusting your desk you will soon start to make everyone around you uncomfortable. Are you modest? Modest people are the salt of the earth. It is possible, however, to be modest to the point of inducing nausea. I believe it was Winston Churchill who once said of an overly modest man, "He must have an awful lot to be modest about." (He said it, of course in more Churchillian phrases.)

Is the difference between enough and too much a difficult one to grasp? Only if you are a fool. Just put yourself in the other fellow's place and imagine how much of these varied virtues you could stand without crying "Enough!" In any event, your beneficiaries will soon make you understand. You don't need a thermometer to measure the warmth of a reaction.

Do not permit the above digression on the dangers of overdoing deter you from doing enough to make your office or shop a place you enjoy coming to. Once you can wake up in the morning without wishing you didn't have to go to work, you have come a long way toward learning to like not only the place in which you work but the work itself as well. At this point we are prepared to face a fact that might not, perhaps, have been acceptable at the beginning of the chapter: a large proportion of the people who do not like their jobs would not like any jobs. Their disaffection is actually directed against the drudgery of work in the generic sense rather than against their own specific work.

It is true that there is in each man and woman a preference for one type of work over all other types. One would rather write for a living than do anything else; another would rather paint than sell; still another would rather sell than pack cartons of merchandise. But those who truly mean it are already doing their favorite work in their spare time. Some will succeed and one day find it possible to devote themselves exclusively to it, while others will not. But all can have the joy of doing what they like best to do for at least a part of the time; and this joy will help to make the work they are *compelled* to do more tolerable.

We live in a great nation. Into its creation went the sweat and toil of countless men and women. Some paved streets, some invented appliances, some typed letters, some shipped cartons, some operated drill presses, some ran errands, some dug sewers, some wrote books, some played music, some planted food, some laid railroad tracks, some painted pictures, some sold groceries. Each one in his own way worked creatively to make a masterpiece of freedom and plenty. Masterpiece though it be, it is not perfect—far from it. There is still much creative work to be done and millions of men and women will keep at the job until there are no more hungry, no more underprivileged, no more discriminated against. Not one of these laborers need feel any lack of pride in his creativity.

If you have a talent that transcends the work you now do every day, try, without risking the loss of your livelihood, to develop it in your spare time. Maybe you will click, maybe you won't. In any event you will experience the joy of trying and doing. At the same time, wipe out your resentment against the work you do for a living. Wipe it out by making your daily place of work one of pleasant and rewarding associations.

If you enjoy *being* there, you will enjoy *working* there.

Chapter Fourteen

I'D CLIMB THE HIGHEST MOUNTAIN

❧ Of all the worlds you live in, the smallest, save the one we shall examine in the final chapter, is your world of friends.

What is a friend? You will never find out by referring to a dictionary. I have before me one of the greatest unabridged dictionaries ever published; and how does this scholarly tome define the word? Thus: *one who entertains for another such sentiments of esteem, respect, and affection, that he seeks his society and welfare.* And that is the *warmest* definition given!

If a friend were no more than that, half the poetry, novels, plays and legends created by man would never have seen the light of day. Damon would not have agreed to take the place of Pythias in prison and risk execution. Let us seek more accurate definitions.

Aristotle said, "A true friend is one soul in two bodies." According to Napoleon, "A faithful friend is the true image of the Deity." Temple called a friend "The greatest medicine." Cicero defined a friend as "A second self." As for Emerson, "A true friend may be reckoned as the masterpiece of nature."

Now we are coming closer to an understanding of what a man means when he says to another, "You are my friend and I am yours." True, we are speaking in terms of the ideal. Friends like Damon and Pythias come once in an era. A true friend who is a masterpiece of nature does not lurk on every street corner. Very few of us ever find a friend so faithful that he is the true image of the Deity. Nevertheless, in our own mundane way, when we speak of friendship we mean something very, very special.

Why is the friendship world so small? The nature of friendship makes it so. Friends are so close, so dear, so demanding, so giving, that it is unlikely that any man could have more than one friend as a friend is defined above. Friendship, unlike love, does not divide without diminishing. A mother can love ten children, giving all of her love to each one. He who offers friendship—ideal friendship—to two or more persons is unable to consummate the offer, for he can give to each only a proportionate fraction of his friendship.

Our own friendship experiences hover somewhere between the dictionary definition and the ideal—closer to the ideal than to the dictionary version, perhaps, but still a long way from the former. Because we do not, in the normal course of our lives, expect to give or to be given on the order of Damon's and Pythias' giving, we need not limit ourselves to a single friend. We can make room in our lives for two friends—sometimes even three —but if we carry it further we are deluding ourselves. We are using the word "friend" to mean "acquaintance." It is a pity to make such a mistake, for even in our own lives, in our own time, it is not unusual for us to be granted the opportunity of experiencing a degree of friendship high enough to make all other relationships except love seem pale.

How do you describe a friend in terms of everyday life? A friend is one who is of your own sex, from whom you need keep no secrets, on whom you can rely for help to the point of severe sacrifice, whose company never palls, to whom you can reveal weakness, from whom you can drink strength, for whom you would do anything in your power, who is always on call when you need him, before whom you are never embarrassed, who understands you and anticipates your words and thoughts, who shares your interests and to reach whom you would climb the highest mountain. It is easy to see that to give and receive all that from more than one or two persons at a time would leave you little time or emotional energy for anything else.

Is it important to have a friend or two in a life full of relatives and neighbors and colleagues and acquaintances and schoolmates? Indeed it is. Friendship is the basic association; all others except love are peripheral. Yet friendship which exists to the exclusion of the other associations tends to become parasitic. You need the leavening influence of the more casual relationships to keep friendship from becoming an unhealthy, obsessive and overly possessive experience.

It is important to have friendship because of the following reasons:

1. Man cannot be without a listening ear. There come times in every person's life when he must confide or burst. The bottled-up person has a bottled-up personality. Sooner or later the man who has no one to whom he can tell everything will have to pay a psychoanalyst to pry it out of the bottle.

2. Man needs someone before whom he can stand figuratively naked and unashamed. He cannot bear to carry alone the burdens of guilt or embarrassment. He can stand so before a friend.

3. Man needs a rock against his doubts and fears, a wall to lean against when he is weak. A friend is a rock and a wall, always dependable, always strong.

4. Man must give as much as he receives or he feels that he is a beneficiary and therefore somehow inferior. A friend demands and receives as much as he gives, so there is always equality between true friends.

5. Man needs someone from whom he can demand and expect to receive that which he wants (within reason, of course) without having to plead for favors. Only on a friend can you make demands. Of others you can make only requests.

6. Man needs periodic relief from the pressures of politeness, tactfulness, sensitivity and guarded expression. With a friend he can find this relief, for a friend does not expect to be met with a façade built by Mrs. Grundy.

7. Man needs someone with whom he can commune in silence, knowing that his presence alone provides the companionship he finds in the presence of a friend.

8. Man needs to know that there is at least one other person in God's world who loves and values him for his soul alone, without bonds of sex, parental or fraternal relationship, dependency in the financial sense, usefulness in a material or career sense. No one but a friend can fill this need. (Some may quarrel with my insistence that a true friend must be of the same sex. That must be a matter of personal opinion. My own observations lead me to believe that the so-called Platonic relationship between a man and a woman cannot long endure in a situation of such intimacy as friendship.)

9. Man needs occasionally a butt for his hostilities and resentments. Only a friend will consent to be such a target. Men without friends sometimes resort to drink: you may have seen one of them staggering along the street, mumbling something like, "I'll show that blankety-blank they can't do that to me, the blankety-blank blank blanks." He is borrowing courage from liquor to hurl his hostilities against the wind.

It is regrettable that there are no guidelines toward the achievement of friendship such as there are in most of the other phases of your life that we have reviewed. How do you make a friend? Who knows? You cannot select a nice person and say to yourself, "I'm going to try to make him my friend." Friendship can only grow out of natural circumstances and as the result of a long period of selective evaluation of many associations in many situations. It cannot be consciously and calculatedly created.

The best you can hope to do is to be ready for friendship when it appears and to know that you cannot have a better friend than you yourself can be. At the same time you must not be so eager for friendship that you flit from prospect to prospect in the hope that this time . . . this time . . . this time you will find it. The danger of such avidity is that you may become the victim of another eager beaver who will imprison you in a demanding relationship which, because you were partly responsible for starting it, you will not have the courage to break.

Truth to tell, people who have the capacity for friendship always have friends. It is never necessary for them to go out on a friend-hunt. Their problem is one of avoiding too many involvements. The probabilities are, therefore, that if you are without the sort of friendship we have discussed, the fault lies in your own personality rather than in the unfavorable operation of the laws of chance. If, as a result of reading these pages, you have been induced to make an effort to improve your personality, you may find it easier than before to find a friend.

Incidentally, it is quite possible to lose a friend, even a friend of long standing. Friends are long-suffering, but these days they are unlikely to suffer unto death. There is a limit and that limit is passed when the demands made on it begin to come out of selfish whim rather than real need. And the loss of a friend can be a devastating, traumatic experience—an experience to be avoided at almost any cost. Indeed, it is worse to lose a friend than not to have one.

When you have alienated a friend you have cast out of your life one who knows all of your most private secrets. It is almost impossible for you to avoid unending worry about that. As long as friendship lasts you have faith in your friend. When friendship breaks and contact is diminished or lost, the sense of confidence becomes progressively weaker. Whenever you meet someone who knows your former friend you wonder how much he knows about you.

When you break with a friend you damage all of your other relationships. The unhappiness that inevitably follows such a parting is carried over into all of your activities and the harm done can persist for years. Also, people who knew of your friendship begin to wonder why it ended and some of them will find reasons for blaming you.

When friendship ends, the therapy to which you have become accustomed ends. Having lost this buffer you either suffer inwardly or start treating your acquaintances and colleagues as you treated your friend while he was a friend. Only friends, as we have indicated, can take such treatment. Others will never stand for it.

It makes much more sense to prevent the death of

friendship. If no one can help you to *find* a friend, it *is* possible to help you to *hold* a friend. Here are a few tips garnered, I confess, from a questionnaire sent out to a group of high school juniors:

1. Never carelessly give away a confidence entrusted by your friend.

2. Don't be a leech.

3. A friend is only human. You must expect her to be different sometimes than she is most of the time and you can't blame her for it.

4. Friends will stand for almost anything but you mustn't lie to them.

5. You can wake a friend in the middle of the night if it is really important, but if you keep doing things like that when it's only trivial they are bound to get tired of it.

6. If you once made a demand on a friend that was granted and then the friend asked you for the same thing and you didn't do it, you have broken the chain of friendship.

7. If you have more than one friend and you give too much attention to one, the other one may resent it.

8. If you did something to break up a friendship you should apologize. If you cry and apologize it is even better. You have to remember your friend is just as unhappy about it as you are and will probably be glad you made an overture.

You couldn't get better advice from college professors than these high school juniors offer.

Chapter Fifteen

YOUR BEST FRIEND IS YOU

You can break every mirror, turn off every light, stand utterly motionless and silent . . . you cannot get away from complete awareness of your own presence. You are always with yourself, your own constant and unrelenting companion. Even when you are doing something else than observing yourself, you know that it is *you* who are doing it. When you are among crowds of friends and acquaintances, you know that it is *you* who are among them. You can get away from people, from places, from problems, from things; you cannot ever, ever get away from yourself.

In this situation isn't it just plain common sense to make a friend of yourself—a good friend, the sort of friend you *like* to be with rather than a disturbing and almost unwelcome permanent guest? There can be no more tragic form of loneliness than that induced by boredom or dissatisfaction with yourself; there can be no more repelling personality than that which reflects repulsion of self. There can be no greater boon than the ability to be joyfully alone with yourself, for if you can be, you will never want for a boon companion: yourself. And if you enjoy your own company it will follow as the night follows the day that others will enjoy it, too.

Now how do you go about making yourself the sort of person and personality you will always enjoy? Is it *possible* to improve your self-image? Well, a wise writer, Aldous Huxley, once said: "There's only one corner of the universe you can be *certain* of improving, and that's your own self." So let us see.

When you are alone you have the choice of a wide variety of activities, interests and diversions: religion, imagination, introspection, education, relaxation, health, philosophy, psychology, talent development, hobbies and memories, to name but a few. There are, indeed, so many things you can do all by yourself that once started on the road to self-improvement, self-sufficiency and self-respect, you run the danger of overdoing the job and becoming a sort of hermit. While it is true that you can be your own best friend, it would be a sad mistake to limit yourself to that one friendship: remember the signal importance of sharing in the quest for genuine happiness.

We shall not attempt here to explore this last-mentioned danger. Rather, we shall assume that you are so eager to enjoy the companionship of many people that your only goal in your effort to improve yourself is to make your life enjoyable when you *must* be alone; and that you will accept as an additional reward for your labors the intensified magnetism you will then exert on others.

The first thing to do is to take a pencil and a pad and list the things which you would like to include in your agenda of self-improvement toward self-liking but which for one reason or another, you have neglected. In a very few minutes you will begin to be amazed at the length of your list and discouraged by the apparent impossibility of following through. There will be the temptation to throw the pencil away and go back to the less complicated pastime of being bored with yourself.

I recall the plaintive wail of a family man of my acquaintance. "You know," he said, "I have a rather full life. I have a family, I have friends and I make a comfortable living. But believe it or not, I'm completely dissatisfied with myself as a person."

"I don't get it," I said. "I thought you loved reading and music and travel and all of the things that make for a well-rounded personality. Why are you dissatisfied?"

He pondered for a moment, then said: "I think, maybe, because I was born too late for a person such as I am. This is too wonderful an age for me. There are so many things to do that I never get *anything* done."

I saw that he was not speaking lightly. His manner was, as usual, tense and somewhat absent, and on his face there was that expression of frustration that is so common among the men and women of today. "Just how do you mean that?" I asked.

"Well," he began, "it's like this. I subscribe to three magazines that I like very much. I belong to a record club that provides me with six stereo recordings per year. I like to keep up with the books of the day and there are a number of old classics I should read. I think I should keep up with the news of the day. I want to see certain plays and movies and there are television and radio programs I like. Then there is my stamp collection to take care of. I have to do some gardening and chores and I have to spend time with my wife and children. I enjoy playing bridge and—"

I took a deep breath. "I get the idea," I said. "So what?"

"So this," he replied. "There are so many things I want to do and so many things I ought to do that I don't know where to begin. I wish I had been born a hundred years ago when life wasn't so complicated."

"I think I understand," I said, "but I don't feel that way at all."

"How come?" he asked. "Aren't we all in the same boat?"

"Maybe we're all in the same boat," I said, "but it's a marvelous boat if you know how to row."

"And I suppose you are an expert rower."

"I am," I said modestly. "You see, I used to drift in the boat just as you are doing, but I got sick and tired of drifting and I decided to do something about it. Now I do so many of the things I like to do that sometimes I think I have invented the forty-eight-hour day."

"You *are* modest," he said.

Then I told him of my solution to the problem that is making so many thousands of good people sick at heart with deprivation and frustration and causing so much nervousness and ill temper and dissatisfaction throughout this land of manifold blessings—and holding them back from the personality improvement and development to which they are entitled.

My solution embodies a simple formula—a formula for enjoying the modern world to the fullest extent possible and for deriving maximum personality benefit. It is divided into three parts:

1. Resignation
2. Selectivity
3. Scheduling

It is as simple as that.

The first part of the formula requires that one recognize and become resigned to the immutable fact that there is so much to be done and experienced in this miraculous twentieth-century world that one cannot possibly do it all. You can't, you just can't read all the good books that come out and all the great books of the past. You can't see all the shows or read all the magazines and newspapers. You can't hear all the music and do all the traveling and participate in all the sports and hear all the lectures and operate all the gadgets and do all of the other things that are available and enjoyable and informative and broadening.

Having recognized and accepted that fact, you begin at once to lose the feeling of guilt that is in some measure at the root of the frustration and tenseness and that bothers you as it bothered my friend; and you are ready to proceed to the second part of the formula, selectivity.

In discussing the matter with my friend after he had accepted point number one, I asked him which were the things he wanted to do more than anything else. This made it necessary for him to become analytical and selective, though not unreasonably so.

"I'd like," he said, "to read twenty best sellers and ten classics every year. I'd like to find time to hear my hi-fi records. I'd like to read my three magazines. I'd like to play bridge at least once a week. There are two one-hour and two half-hour television programs I wouldn't want to miss. I'd like to take half a dozen weekend drives a year. I'd like to keep up with my stamp collection. I'd like to see about five hit shows and attend five concerts every season. I'd like to get some piano practice in. I'd like to brush up on my high school French. I'd like to be able on occasion to visit friends with my wife and have them visit us in turn. I'd like to spend some time with my children."

"Would you be happier if you could manage to do all that?" I asked.

"I'll say I would," he replied. "Not only happier, but more satisfied with myself. But you see how hopeless it is. There isn't that much time in the world."

"Yes, there is," I said. "We are now ready for the third step, scheduling."

We translated his desires into hours as follows:

Books. The average book can be read in about three hours. In ninety hours he could read the thirty books at which he aimed.

Hi-fi. He wanted to listen to his recordings for at least two hours a week. Leaving out the hottest months of the summer, his listening would consume about eighty-eight hours a year.

Magazines. He wanted to give them as much time as he gave his recordings—another eighty-eight hours.

Television. The four television programs he liked took up three hours a week for ten months, or 132 hours a year.

Stamps. He thought an hour a week would do the job. That would mean forty-four hours a year if the two hot summer months were omitted.

French. About half an hour four times a week would be needed for brushing up. Add eighty-eight hours.

Piano. He felt that this would require the same time as his French study—eighty-eight hours.

And that was it—all the things he wanted to do and never seemed to have the time for could be done in 618 hours of organized time out of the 8,760 hours in a year!

I was pleased with the results of my calculations, but my friend was not easily sold. "Sure," he said, "it sounds easy—only 618 hours out of 8,760, but you've included in the latter number all the sleeping hours, all the working hours, all the visiting and theatre hours and all the concert hours. Let's see how it comes out when you aren't so tricky with the figures."

For a moment I thought he had me. Sleep and work alone required 4,800 or more of the total. Then there was an evening every week for bridge—another 175 hours in 44 weeks. He wanted to see about five shows a year, go to five concerts, give ten parties and attend ten parties. Calculated at the rate of four hours an evening, these activities would consume 120 hours. He had left now about 3,665 out of which to snatch the 618.

"I ask you now," I said, "does the program still seem impossible?"

"No," he admitted at last. "I'm beginning to think it can be done."

It can be done. What is required is the conviction that it can and the willingness to give the required amount of time to each activity. You can set a rigid schedule for each day or week, or you can hop from activity to activity as the mood comes upon you. It doesn't matter how you go about it as long as you maintain determination, a sense of purpose and an understanding of the actualities of time.

In my friend's case it worked out very well. One of his favorite television programs was a Sunday telecast; a great deal of his socializing was normally done on weekends; some of his concerts and theatres were Saturday night events; a fair amount of his book reading was done during the summer months. This left many four-evening weeks (one night was reserved for bridge) during which he could pursue a full and satisfying schedule which, when the year was over, gave him even more than I had promised.

In the beginning he had expressed some concern about the possibility that if he followed my advice he would be depriving his wife and children of the time and attention to which they were entitled. As he went forward, however, he found that in addition to the dinner hour they spent together each evening, he was able to be with them a great deal on weekends and in the summer months. Moreover, he found that he could include them in much of his schedule of self-improvement. They could listen while he played his recordings, they could sing along when he played the piano and they, too, could learn a bit of French while he was reviewing the language. Often, too, he would read aloud to them from the books and magazines.

In short, it worked out fine. "You know," he said, "this has taught me something about time. Time is relative. When you are frittering your time away there are only twelve hours in a day. When you are using your time successfully, there are forty-eight hours in a day."

He was quite right. Time should not be measured by the ticking of a clock but rather by what we do with it and what it gives us. When you use your allotted time properly you actually put so much more into life and get so much more out of it that in a sense you may consider that you live longer.

It is possible that none of the above applies to you. Perhaps your problem is not so much that you have too wide a spread of interests to cope with as that your range of interests is too narrow. It is conceivable that you spend most of your spare time before the TV because you *prefer* that pastime to anything else. I would not want to be misjudged. I am not anti-TV. I think it is one of the greatest marvels of our age, with a tremendous potential as a personality development aid if properly utilized and selectively employed. The evil that can be wrought by television is due to the ease with which one can drift into using it as an eternal escape from life and from striving; and if you are a TV addict to the exclusion of more creative effort of your own, you are abusing not only this marvelous product of human ingenuity but yourself as well. And if you belong to that ever-growing coterie of TV hounds who spend their evenings watching the screen and their days rehashing the previous evening's programs, you are deliberately excluding yourself from acceptance by people who are far more interesting, far more creative and far more popular.

Get out of the TV rut. Start doing and learning things yourself instead of watching the diminutive screen images of others who do and learn them. If nothing else interests you strongly, try doing something broadening despite your lack of interest. Appreciation of the better things in life (in the cultural area) does not come easily or naturally—it has to be acquired and developed. We enjoy jazz or rock and roll before we have grown up to opera and symphonic music; we delight in photographic paintings before we can understand and love impressionistic and nonobjective advances in art; we can appreciate detective stories before we can grasp great literature.

"Well," you may say, "why should I struggle to understand such things when I can get just as much pleasure out of the things I already understand?"

The answer, without derogating rock and roll, detective stories, photographic art and the like, is that the pleasure derived from the more highly developed cultural forms is far greater and far more gratifying than you can imagine. Moreover, since the higher forms are loved and appreciated by humanity's elite, your own familiarity and appreciation of them can carry you to the top rungs of social intercourse. The simple, elementary forms of culture were originally for savages. From the bongo-bongo drums man developed simple scales and instruments for making simple music. From these or their equivalent he advanced to the subtleties of more highly developed music. In each stage of advancement there were many who were content to remain with the simplest forms of music of their eras and a few who tired of their simplicity and inanity and sought new means of expressing their now more highly developed taste and understanding. And so it was with art and other forms of creative expression.

It is said by people who are authorities that the simple things, that can be instantly understood and appreciated, very quickly pall, while the more complex things, that have to be studied and lived with and observed before understanding comes, provide unending delight. It may have happened to you that you once saw a painting that you fell in love with at sight and had to have. You took it home and in a very short time you tired of it. On the other hand, you may have passed a painting in a window that at first struck you as involved and meaningless. The next time you passed by you caught a flash of something—you didn't know just what—that made you stop and look more closely. The next time you saw still more to study and each time thereafter the painting took on more and more meaning and gave you more and more pleasure. That, friend, was you in the process of development. A painting like that would be a joy to you forever.

Get hold of your local adult education program. Study it for a course in a language, or in art or the appreciation of art, or in music or its appreciation, or in history, or in psychology, or in comparative religion, or in anthropology, or in literature. If one of the courses appeals to you, enroll. If you find nothing you would like to study, close your eyes and let a pencil point fall on any course it chooses to strike. Stick to the course for a year, come what may. You will probably find it boring and unrewarding at first. Stick to it. Sooner or later it will start to take hold of you, to grow on you. Sooner or later you will find yourself able to talk about it, to the surprise and admiration of your friends. That one course will be your opening wedge to further exploration. Appreciation of culture is indivisible; once you become the sort of person who has risen out of simplicity in one area, you will be dissatisfied with the elementary in all areas. You will be entering the ranks of the elite.

Join one of the book clubs devoted to the classics or to the less popular novels, or, if you wish, to the best sellers of the day. Read the first few books through to the end, whether you enjoy them or not. Sooner or later you will start enjoying them and preferring them to trash.

Go to concerts and lectures even if they bore you to tears. If you have even the faintest trace of intelligence the time will come when you will not only enjoy them but criticize and compare them as to merit as well.

If you have been a stick-in-the-mud, take a trip to another country even if you have to borrow the money and eat less lavishly in order to repay it. (Incidentally, costs of charter flights and group reservations are now so low that anyone who is employed at a salary even slightly higher than needed for the necessities of life can afford them.) A person who has visited another land has become tremendously interesting to those who have not; he will find, too, that he has much to exchange with those who have.

To repeat: we live in a marvelous age. *Live* in it? Too many of us merely *exist* in it. What a waste it is to have such a wealth of experiences, treasures, creative fruits and adventures at the tips of our fingers and to go through life without ever reaching out for them!

Don't be an oyster in a shell; it can get awfully lonely and boring and miserable in there. Step out of the shell and take a look at the glorious world. It's yours for the taking if you want to take it and if you dare to take it.

And once you start to soar you will be in the most heavenly company. It never gets lonely up there.

MELVIN POWERS SELF-IMPROVEMENT LIBRARY

JUST FOR WOMEN

____ COSMOPOLITAN'S GUIDE TO MARVELOUS MEN Foreword by *Helen Gurley Brown*   3.00
____ COSMOPOLITAN'S HANG-UP HANDBOOK Foreword by *Helen Gurley Brown*   4.00
____ COSMOPOLITAN'S LOVE BOOK—A GUIDE TO ECSTASY IN BED   7.00
____ COSMOPOLITAN'S NEW ETIQUETTE GUIDE Foreword by *Helen Gurley Brown*   4.00
____ I AM A COMPLEAT WOMAN *Doris Hagopian & Karen O'Connor Sweeney*   3.00
____ JUST FOR WOMEN—A GUIDE TO THE FEMALE BODY *Richard E. Sand, M.D.*   5.00
____ NEW APPROACHES TO SEX IN MARRIAGE *John E. Eichenlaub, M.D.*   3.00
____ SEXUALLY ADEQUATE FEMALE *Frank S. Caprio, M.D.*   3.00
____ SEXUALLY FULFILLED WOMAN *Dr. Rachel Copelan*   5.00
____ YOUR FIRST YEAR OF MARRIAGE *Dr. Tom McGinnis*   3.00

MARRIAGE, SEX & PARENTHOOD

____ ABILITY TO LOVE *Dr. Allan Fromme*   7.00
____ GUIDE TO SUCCESSFUL MARRIAGE *Drs. Albert Ellis & Robert Harper*   7.00
____ HOW TO RAISE AN EMOTIONALLY HEALTHY, HAPPY CHILD *Albert Ellis, Ph.D.*   7.00
____ PARENT SURVIVAL TRAINING *Marvin Silverman, Ed.D. & David Lustig, Ph.D.*   10.00
____ SEX WITHOUT GUILT *Albert Ellis, Ph.D.*   5.00
____ SEXUALLY ADEQUATE MALE *Frank S. Caprio, M.D.*   3.00
____ SEXUALLY FULFILLED MAN *Dr. Rachel Copelan*   5.00
____ STAYING IN LOVE *Dr. Norton F. Kristy*   7.00

MELVIN POWERS' MAIL ORDER LIBRARY

____ HOW TO GET RICH IN MAIL ORDER *Melvin Powers*   20.00
____ HOW TO WRITE A GOOD ADVERTISEMENT *Victor O. Schwab*   20.00
____ MAIL ORDER MADE EASY *J. Frank Brumbaugh*   20.00

METAPHYSICS & OCCULT

____ BOOK OF TALISMANS, AMULETS & ZODIACAL GEMS *William Pavitt*   7.00
____ CONCENTRATION—A GUIDE TO MENTAL MASTERY *Mouni Sadhu*   7.00
____ EXTRA-TERRESTRIAL INTELLIGENCE—THE FIRST ENCOUNTER   6.00
____ FORTUNE TELLING WITH CARDS *P. Foli*   5.00
____ HOW TO INTERPRET DREAMS, OMENS & FORTUNE TELLING SIGNS *Gettings*   5.00
____ HOW TO UNDERSTAND YOUR DREAMS *Geoffrey A. Dudley*   5.00
____ IN DAYS OF GREAT PEACE *Mouni Sadhu*   3.00
____ MAGICIAN—HIS TRAINING AND WORK *W. E. Butler*   5.00
____ MEDITATION *Mouni Sadhu*   7.00
____ MODERN NUMEROLOGY *Morris C. Goodman*   5.00
____ NUMEROLOGY—ITS FACTS AND SECRETS *Ariel Yvon Taylor*   5.00
____ NUMEROLOGY MADE EASY *W. Mykian*   5.00
____ PALMISTRY MADE EASY *Fred Gettings*   5.00
____ PALMISTRY MADE PRACTICAL *Elizabeth Daniels Squire*   5.00
____ PALMISTRY SECRETS REVEALED *Henry Frith*   4.00
____ PROPHECY IN OUR TIME *Martin Ebon*   2.50
____ SUPERSTITION—ARE YOU SUPERSTITIOUS? *Eric Maple*   2.00
____ TAROT *Mouni Sadhu*   10.00
____ TAROT OF THE BOHEMIANS *Papus*   7.00
____ WAYS TO SELF-REALIZATION *Mouni Sadhu*   7.00
____ WITCHCRAFT, MAGIC & OCCULTISM—A FASCINATING HISTORY *W. B. Crow*   7.00
____ WITCHCRAFT—THE SIXTH SENSE *Justine Glass*   7.00
____ WORLD OF PSYCHIC RESEARCH *Hereward Carrington*   2.00

SELF-HELP & INSPIRATIONAL

____ CHARISMA—HOW TO GET "THAT SPECIAL MAGIC" *Marcia Grad*	7.00
____ DAILY POWER FOR JOYFUL LIVING *Dr. Donald Curtis*	7.00
____ DYNAMIC THINKING *Melvin Powers*	5.00
____ GREATEST POWER IN THE UNIVERSE *U. S. Andersen*	7.00
____ GROW RICH WHILE YOU SLEEP *Ben Sweetland*	7.00
____ GROWTH THROUGH REASON *Albert Ellis, Ph.D.*	7.00
____ GUIDE TO PERSONAL HAPPINESS *Albert Ellis, Ph.D. & Irving Becker, Ed.D.*	7.00
____ HANDWRITING ANALYSIS MADE EASY *John Marley*	7.00
____ HANDWRITING TELLS *Nadya Olyanova*	7.00
____ HOW TO ATTRACT GOOD LUCK *A.H.Z. Carr*	7.00
____ HOW TO BE GREAT *Dr. Donald Curtis*	5.00
____ HOW TO DEVELOP A WINNING PERSONALITY *Martin Panzer*	7.00
____ HOW TO DEVELOP AN EXCEPTIONAL MEMORY *Young & Gibson*	5.00
____ HOW TO LIVE WITH A NEUROTIC *Albert Ellis, Ph.D.*	7.00
____ HOW TO OVERCOME YOUR FEARS *M. P. Leahy, M.D.*	3.00
____ HOW TO SUCCEED *Brian Adams*	7.00
____ HUMAN PROBLEMS & HOW TO SOLVE THEM *Dr. Donald Curtis*	5.00
____ I CAN *Ben Sweetland*	7.00
____ I WILL *Ben Sweetland*	3.00
____ KNIGHT IN THE RUSTY ARMOR *Robert Fisher*	5.00
____ LEFT-HANDED PEOPLE *Michael Barsley*	5.00
____ MAGIC IN YOUR MIND *U.S. Andersen*	7.00
____ MAGIC OF THINKING BIG *Dr. David J. Schwartz*	3.00
____ MAGIC OF THINKING SUCCESS *Dr. David J. Schwartz*	7.00
____ MAGIC POWER OF YOUR MIND *Walter M. Germain*	7.00
____ MENTAL POWER THROUGH SLEEP SUGGESTION *Melvin Powers*	3.00
____ NEVER UNDERESTIMATE THE SELLING POWER OF A WOMAN *Dottie Walters*	7.00
____ NEW GUIDE TO RATIONAL LIVING *Albert Ellis, Ph.D. & R. Harper, Ph.D.*	7.00
____ PSYCHO-CYBERNETICS *Maxwell Maltz, M.D.*	7.00
____ PSYCHOLOGY OF HANDWRITING *Nadya Olyanova*	7.00
____ SALES CYBERNETICS *Brian Adams*	7.00
____ SCIENCE OF MIND IN DAILY LIVING *Dr. Donald Curtis*	7.00
____ SECRET OF SECRETS *U.S. Andersen*	7.00
____ SECRET POWER OF THE PYRAMIDS *U. S. Andersen*	7.00
____ SELF-THERAPY FOR THE STUTTERER *Malcolm Frazer*	3.00
____ SUCCESS-CYBERNETICS *U. S. Andersen*	7.00
____ 10 DAYS TO A GREAT NEW LIFE *William E. Edwards*	3.00
____ THINK AND GROW RICH *Napoleon Hill*	7.00
____ THREE MAGIC WORDS *U. S. Andersen*	7.00
____ TREASURY OF COMFORT *Edited by Rabbi Sidney Greenberg*	7.00
____ TREASURY OF THE ART OF LIVING *Sidney S. Greenberg*	7.00
____ WHAT YOUR HANDWRITING REVEALS *Albert E. Hughes*	4.00
____ YOUR SUBCONSCIOUS POWER *Charles M. Simmons*	7.00
____ YOUR THOUGHTS CAN CHANGE YOUR LIFE *Dr. Donald Curtis*	7.00

The books listed above can be obtained from your book dealer or directly from Melvin Powers.
When ordering, please remit $1.50 postage for the first book and 50¢ for each additional book.

Melvin Powers
12015 Sherman Road, No. Hollywood, California 91605